GARDEN UP!

Smart Vertical Gardening for Small and Large Spaces

SUSAN MORRISON & REBECCA SWEET

Published by Cool Springs Press
P. O. Box 2828, Brentwood, Tennessee 37204

Library of Congress Cataloging-in-Publication Data

Morrison, Susan, 1963-
Garden up! : smart vertical gardening for small and large spaces / Susan Morrison and Rebecca Sweet.
p. cm.
Includes index.
ISBN 978-1-59186-492-9 (softcover)
1. Vertical gardening. I. Sweet, Rebecca. II. Title. III. Title: Smart vertical gardening for small and large spaces.

SB463.5.M67 2011
635--dc22

2010046528

EAN: 9781591864929

First Printing 2011
Printed in the United States of America
10 9 8 7 6 5 4 3 2

Managing Editor: Billie Brownell, Cover to Cover Editorial Services
Copyeditor: Jennifer Greenstein
Art Director: Sheri Ferguson, Ferguson Design Studio

Cover photos by Rob Cardillo. Cover garden designs by (from left) Fox Hollow Design, Thomas Hobbs and Gasper Landscape Design.

Visit the Cool Springs Press website at www.coolspringspress.com.
You can find this title, other Cool Springs Press books, and other gardening books for sale at www.GardenBookstore.net.

GARDEN **UP!**

Growing Successful Gardeners™
www.coolspringspress.com
Brentwood, Tennessee

Smart Vertical Gardening for Small and Large Spaces

SUSAN MORRISON & REBECCA SWEET

Acknowledgements & Dedications

This book could not have been written without the generous assistance of so many talented gardeners, designers, and writers. To all of the friends we have made through the Association of Professional Landscape Designers, Master Gardener groups, Blogging, Flickr, Facebook, and Twitter: thank you for your support and expertise! Likewise, we are deeply indebted to our wonderful clients, many of whom not only allowed us to photograph their gardens, but who gamely acted as guinea pigs as we experimented with new ideas.

We especially wish to acknowledge the following individuals, for sharing their knowledge, firing our creativity, and opening their gardens and nurseries to us: Angela Davis, Patrick Fizgerald, Emily Goodman, Jayme Jenkins, Theresa Loe, Lennart and Carla Lundstrom, Jim Martin, Kerry Michaels, Lisa Mitchell, Pam Penick, Jenny Peterson, Laura Schaub, Robin Stockwell, and Freeland and Sabrina Tanner.

To my husband Nicholas Bowerman, who didn't blink an eye when I naively declared writing a book sounded like a fun project, and who proceeded to support me cheerfully through every hair-pulling moment.

—*Susan*

To Tom and Emily, for willingly eating a summer's worth of frozen dinners while providing endless support and patience. Lots and lots of patience. To Michael and his 24/7 tech support. And to my mother, father, and grandmother, whose love of gardening provide me with unlimited inspiration.

—*Rebecca*

Invasive Plants

An invasive plant is defined as any nonnative plant that adversely affects the habitat it invades. Left unchecked, invasive plants can overwhelm native vegetation, harbor pests that are harmful to other plants, and even alter the genetic makeup of native species. Tens of millions of dollars are spent each year in an effort to control the damage done by invasive species.

While some plants that have invasive root systems, such as culinary mint, may be controlled by planting in containers, keep in mind that many plants propagate by seed. Even if you are vigilant about controlling new shoots or seedlings in your own garden, wind, birds, or animals can spread seeds many miles away.

Because vastly different cultural conditions may exist between one region and another, a plant that is well behaved in one part of the country may be invasive in another. Therefore, a plant's inclusion in this book is not a guarantee that it's suitable for your area. To ensure you've made a good choice, check with your state's invasive plant list before planting any species you are unfamiliar with.

Noninvasive in dry, western climates, Berberis thunbergii *has invaded open spaces in over twenty states throughout the Midwest and Northwest, where it has caused significant damage.*

Introduction

Why Garden Up?

When you hear the phrase "vertical gardening," what comes to mind? You might think about roses scrambling up a trellis, or an overhead arbor dripping with wisteria. Those in search of a more contemporary style may envision a mosaic of succulents hung on an outdoor wall, while edible gardeners see a riotous mix of creative containers, with tomatoes and peas reaching for the sun. Perhaps you garden on a balcony or in a narrow backyard and gardening up is your secret weapon to getting the most out of a small space.

Vertical gardening is all of these things and more. Whether you need help solving a specific problem or are in search of inspiration, this book will show you how to take your landscape to the next level by maximizing vertical spaces. The good news is you don't have to be an expert gardener to take advantage of this exciting trend. We've tapped into our combined twenty years of experience as garden designers to share our best design strategies, plant choices, and how-to advice. *Garden Up!* is packed with inspiring and informative photos as well as a feature we call Design Spotlight that points out specific vertical gardening solutions. For the do-it-yourselfer, we've included several projects that can be accomplished in a day or a weekend.

Although vertical gardening is a relatively new term, people have long been taking advantage of vertical spaces. Incorporating an arbor or trellis is still one of the easiest and most effective ways to add a third dimension to your landscape. Chapter 1, "Arbors and Trellises," shows you how these timeless garden structures can increase curb appeal, carve out intimate spaces, or tame unruly gardens. You will also find our tips for selecting the right arbor or trellis for your home.

While it might be true that "thin is in," most people prefer to have planting beds that are deep enough to accommodate a mix of shrubs and flowering plants. Yet even the largest gardens usually have an awkward spot or two that defy traditional planting techniques. In chapter 2, "Skinny Spaces," we share some of our favorite design strategies for narrow areas and introduce you to a whole new way of thinking about layers in a garden bed. We even tackle the ultimate skinny spaces: long and narrow side yards.

Chapter 3, "Garden Secrets," might just as easily have been named "Eyesores Galore"! Whether it's an ugly chimney, a boxy air-conditioning unit, or a neighborhood utility pole, almost every yard or garden has something you wish would just disappear. While we can't cross our arms and blink them away, "Garden Secrets" offers suggestions on how to disguise some of the most common visual problems that homeowners deal with.

Architectural plants and carefully chosen vertical elements turn a tiny space into a lush, tropical retreat.

Chapter 4, "Urban Gardens," addresses the unique set of challenges those who garden on small balconies or in tiny courtyards face. Whether it's finding space, choosing a container, or designing a focal-point wall, we offer a range of vertical approaches to turn these often underused spaces into cozy urban retreats.

Although no one can deny the appeal of a garden brimming with colorful ornamental plants, what is more satisfying than preparing a meal from ingredients harvested from your own vegetable garden? Chapter 5, "Edibles," is all about growing your own produce, and you'll be amazed at how big your harvest can be if you grow up instead of out.

In many ways, chapter 6, "Living Walls," is the heart of this book. Inspired by the incredible vertical gardens popping up in public spaces such as parks, schools, and public buildings all over the country, in this chapter we not only show you the mechanics of a living wall, but share a range of do-it-yourself options geared toward the rest of us.

What gardening book would be complete without at least one chapter devoted to plants? In chapter 7, "Plant Picks," we've put together a select list of plant recommendations, each addressing a specific situation vertical gardeners face. We've even included a bonus section of planting plans that highlight some of our favorite container combinations to give you even more ideas.

Writing this book has given us the opportunity to peek into gardens of all shapes and sizes. We've been inspired, amazed, amused, and delighted at the ingenious ways gardeners all over the country have incorporated vertical elements into their landscapes, whether they garden on a multiacre estate in Napa Valley or on a tiny balcony in the suburbs of Austin, Texas.

Arbors and trellises are much more than handy structures for training vines or easy solutions for a blank wall or fence. Besides offering small-space gardeners another place to garden, they can add significant curb appeal to your home. In larger landscapes, they act as room dividers

ARBORS AND TRELLISES

and focal points. And in landscapes of any size, they help define intimate spaces. Elegant or ornate, traditional or contemporary, arbors and trellises are one of the easiest ways to add a third dimension to your garden.

Front Yard Arbors

Welcoming Guests to Your Home

Have you ever heard the saying "You never get a second chance to make a first impression"? Not only does this wise advice apply to job interviews or the first day of school, but it applies to your home as well. A front yard is more than just a green area separating your house from the sidewalk; it's a multifunctional space that marks the transition from the outdoors to the indoors, a place to greet visitors and to say your good-byes, and an opportunity to complement your home. It's also a chance to express a little of your personality! Of the many elements that contribute to a front yard's curb appeal, a thoughtfully placed arbor is one of the easiest ways to make your front yard more inviting.

A natural transition occurs when visitors come to your home. Designers use the term "entry sequence" to refer to the path from public spaces (the street or sidewalk) to the semiprivate or private space closer to your home's front door. A well-planned entry sequence connects a house to the landscape and creates a cohesive space. Ideally, this path to the front door is easily identified, complements the home's exterior, and combines with other landscape elements to create a pleasant walking experience.

Indoors, it's easy to understand the difference between common areas and private ones: archways, room dividers, and doors that open and close make it clear where one room ends and another begins. Outdoor boundaries and edges aren't necessarily as well defined; adding an arbor is one way to mark transitions outside.

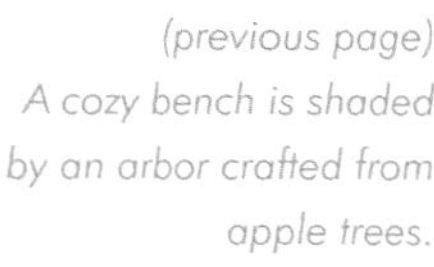

(previous page) A cozy bench is shaded by an arbor crafted from apple trees.

A rose-covered arbor welcomes visitors to this garden.

(facing page) An arbor is an easy way to add curb appeal to your home.

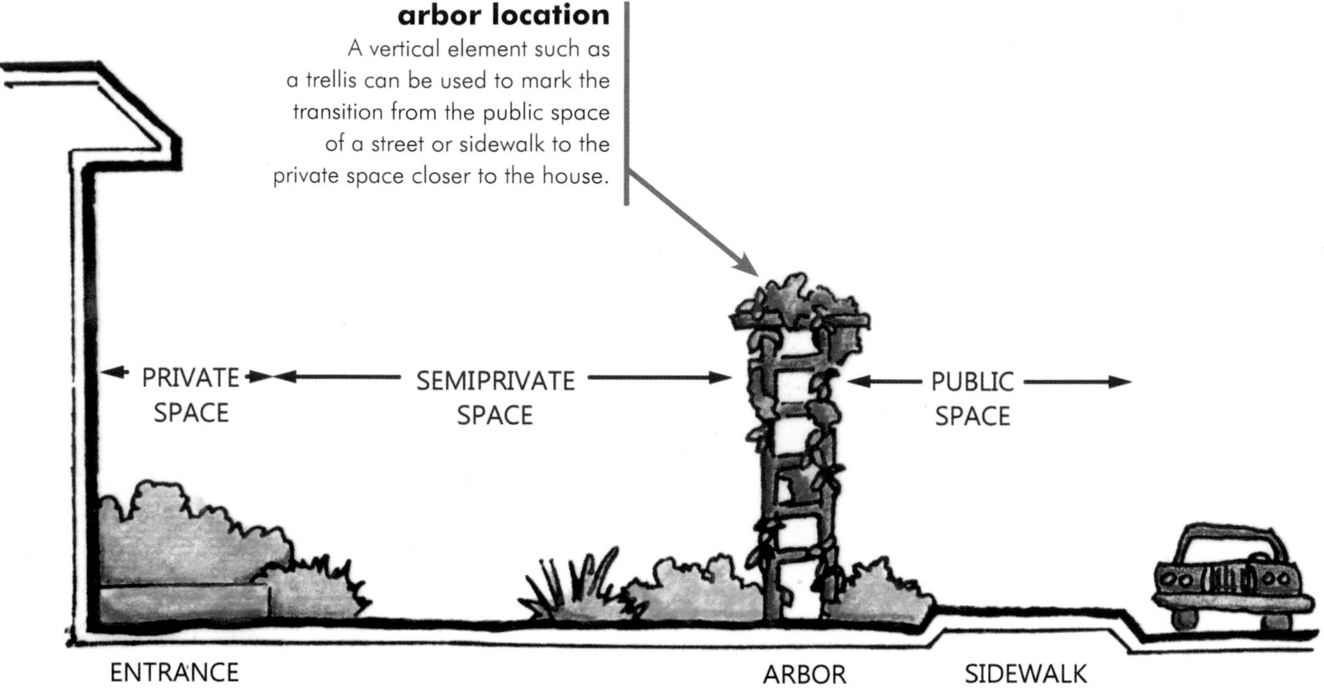

Locating an Arbor

An arbor will have a different impact depending on where it is placed. Arbors can be positioned where the main path meets the sidewalk, closer to the home, or even right against the exterior of the house. If it's at the entrance to the yard or path, an arbor gives the signal that this is a more private space. An arbor that is gated or is part of a fence gives an even stronger impression that the front yard is a semiprivate area. For smaller front yards, placing an arbor close to the path's beginning makes sense, as the distance from the street to the front door means the transition from public space to private space happens almost immediately.

These days, many people have little use for a traditional lawn, opting instead to transform a front yard into a garden. Of course, a garden is a much more personal space than an expanse of lawn and may even include room for seating or for displaying outdoor art or accessories. Placing an arbor at the entrance to your front yard garden is an excellent way to tell visitors that they are entering a more private area, intended for invited guests only.

Seasonal Interest

A planted arbor lets you bring a warm jolt of seasonal color to your front yard whether you choose plants such as a wisteria to usher in spring or Boston ivy to mark the cooler days of fall. Even after a vine has gone dormant, an arbor will be there to welcome visitors to your home.

Along the Path

If your front yard is larger, consider placing an arbor farther along the path. This helps to extend the transitional zone and makes a walk to the front door more interesting and pleasant.

A front yard dominated by lawn and shrubs can be a missed opportunity to tap into your landscape's potential. Outdoor foyers or courtyards not only make the front of your home more attractive, but also create a space that can be used for a range of activities, such as dining, visiting with friends, or simply relaxing. Adding an arbor as an entry point to a partly secluded space enhances privacy and is an excellent way to reclaim an otherwise unused front yard.

The entrance to this courtyard is clearly defined.

An arbor separates a cozy seating area from the street.

Stucco walls painted in warm colors form a dramatic backdrop for pastel climbing roses.

The colors of the 'Sally Holmes' rose range from soft apricot to a creamy white.

Architectural Detail

Arbors or trellises added right at the door contribute both architectural detail and soften a home's exterior with green and growing plants. Choose a trellis that complements your home's style and make sure the structure and weight are solid enough to stand up to its architectural design. A delicate arbor painted white and planted with flowering vines might be enough to highlight the simple lines and homey feel of a bungalow or cottage. In contrast, the Mediterranean-style homes popular throughout the Southwest are better matched by trellises built from classic materials like dark-stained wood or wrought iron.

Maximize Curb Appeal

Complement the Landscape

For a homeowner interested in more gardening opportunities, the chance to acquire additional growing space is one of the main attractions of incorporating an arbor or trellis into a front garden. But its value goes beyond the opportunity to add more greenery. Besides welcoming visitors to your home, garden structures like these are a terrific way to increase your front yard's curb appeal.

For most homes, doors and entryways are located at the front of the house, right where we'd expect to find them. When the main entrance is on the side of the house, however, visitors may not know where to go. Front doors that are approached from an unexpected direction, like the driveway, can also cause confusion. Highlighting the path with an arbor is an easy way to make it more prominent and guide visitors to the entrance.

A charming arbor guides visitors to the hidden front door.

An arbor marks the location of an untraditional side entrance.

In general, the elements that make up your front yard landscape should be chosen with the architecture of your home in mind. Whether your home has an identifiable architectural style, such as Victorian or ranch, or simply a strong character, as in modern or traditional homes, the right arbor will help create an integrated, cohesive landscape. If you're not sure what style is right for you, look to your home for clues. Repeating elements of your house in the front yard is one of the easiest ways to ensure a unified space. For example, homes with details such as carved wooden shutters or doors are usually complemented by those materials repeated in the landscape. Similarly, European-style homes accented with wrought-iron window boxes might be enhanced by an arbor made of metal.

Use Arbors to Direct the View

No matter how much time you spend making your landscape beautiful, for many homes the dominant front yard feature will still be the driveway and garage. Fortunately, arbors do more than mark pathways. With its visual appeal and significant scale, an arbor becomes a focal point. A well-placed arbor draws the eye, taking the focus off a bland expanse of oversized driveway and putting it on the house and garden.

Garden Rooms

Getting From Here to There

Professional designers and home gardeners alike love the concept of "garden rooms," as they provide an attractive, effective way to organize a space. Gardens sometimes suffer from a lack of separation, with patio furniture, planting beds, and swing sets all mixed together in one big open space. A backyard like this can overwhelm the eye and prevent you from getting the most out of your space.

Inside the house, we rely on walls, ceilings, and doors to separate one room from the next. Outside, gardeners hope to achieve the same effect with a mix of hardscape, lawn, and planting beds. But remember, the ground plane is one-dimensional. We know from experience that the only way to create a backyard that flows from room to room is to think three-dimensionally. That means using walls, ceilings, and doors—or at least the illusion of them—to define outdoor rooms. How to achieve this depends on the size of your garden, the activities you enjoy, and the atmosphere you want to create.

The color and materials of this arbor reflect the style of the home.

A rustic arbor marks the entrance to another part of the garden.

People want their backyards to accommodate a whole range of requirements, from leisure activities like dining, entertaining, and kids' play to practical needs like storage and growing vegetables. This means that a backyard that gets used regularly (the kind we like best) can quickly become cluttered. Dividing your backyard into a series of garden rooms will help keep the space from becoming overwhelming.

Begin by determining how to organize your rooms. For most people, dividing the landscape into functional activities is the best approach. For example, a typical backyard might have a place for dining, a space for relaxing, a play area, and even a spot for growing herbs, vegetables, or fruit. Besides making it a more interesting and intimate place, organizing your garden functionally allows you to set the tone from one room to the next. An area set aside for reading and relaxing can be made more tranquil with the addition of comfortable cushions and fragrant plants. A vegetable garden might include a potting station and informal gravel paths.

A crescent-shaped planting bed helps define this garden's rooms.

Garden Nooks

If your backyard is small, you might think transforming it into a series of rooms will make it feel even smaller, but in fact, the opposite is true. When everything is clearly visible in one quick glance, the result is a space that can feel cramped. In contrast, a garden separated into different areas, even subtly, creates a sense of destination and an overall impression of a larger space.

While it's seldom practical in a small space to completely separate one area from another, a series of connected nooks partially separated by plants or garden structures brings a touch of mystery and discovery, and results in a garden that is both intimate and integrated. This means letting go of traditional notions of planting only around the perimeter of the garden and instead mingling plants and seating throughout. Although vertical plants can be used to help separate one part of the garden from another, we find arbors to be a particularly effective way to define a garden nook.

In this large garden, an arbor provides a sense of scale so the bench is not lost in the landscape.

Overhead arbors are both practical and effective for defining the most important rooms in a garden. Whether that's an outdoor dining room or a comfortable seating arrangement, a ceiling helps identify the space as one of the centerpieces of the garden and provides protection from sun, rain, and wind. While adding structures like these is a good idea, be careful not to inadvertently lose the sense of being in a garden. Include plenty of green and growing things.

The arbor above this hammock creates a private nook within a larger garden.

In a small garden, rooms can be as intimate as you choose. A tiny patio furnished with a simple bistro table or a hammock tucked beneath an arbor is enough to create the illusion of a separate space and increase both its beauty and functionality.

The overhead arbor encloses a seating area, while vertical plants soften the space.

Arbors help define transitions within a larger garden.

Taming a Large Garden

In larger landscapes, garden rooms may be defined by borders, by entrances, or by both. In a smaller garden, rooms might be only casually separated, but in a large backyard, strong vertical elements are generally needed to bring a sense of order. Viewable from a distance, vertical structures act as road signs, pulling you through the garden and signaling that something new or interesting lies beyond.

Arbors are particularly effective at announcing the entrance to a new room, whether this is a major transition, as in the movement from formal gardens to less cultivated areas, or a minor transition, as in the movement from open space to a room with a specific purpose such as a vegetable garden. In a large space, defining multiple rooms with strong borders can create a cluttered effect. In contrast, borders and walls that continue from one room to the next provide continuity and unity in a garden, so that the simple addition of an arbor or archway is all that is needed to define a new space.

DESIGN SPOTLIGHT

Garden Transitions

When Rebecca remodeled her garden shed into an office, she wanted her garden to reflect the distinction between downtime and work time. This artfully placed rose arbor not only signals a clear transition from home to office, but frames a charming view in both directions and acts as a seasonal focal point.

Break Time—Although Rebecca considers the office her workspace, a nearby bench creates a comfortable area to take a break and enjoy a different view of the garden.

Long-blooming 'Fourth of July' roses add seasonal interest to the garden.

Once the roses go dormant, details like this intricate medallion ensure the arbor remains a focal point year-round.

The rose arbor separates the main garden from the office located beyond.

Japanese forest grass (Hakonechloa macra 'Aureola') provides contrasting texture and color for the traditional rose arbor and reinforces the arbor's symmetry.

Arbors and other vertical elements are not only effective as room dividers, but are ideal for carving intimate spaces out of larger ones. It can be challenging to add a human scale to expansive gardens. The addition of a bench or small patio can easily backfire, as small-scale seating adrift in an oversize area may lack intimacy or connection to its surroundings. Nestling a bench or table under an arbor creates a comfortable sense of scale. This will not only make your garden more inviting, but also result in a charming scene that can serve as a focal point in your garden.

A bench at the end of this vegetable garden invites visitors to meander over and have a seat.

A bench sits beneath an arbor crafted from espaliered apple trees.

Choosing an Arbor or Trellis

Elements of Style

Vibrant trumpet vine (Distictis buccinatoria) is a good choice for large-sized structures.

There are many things to consider when choosing an arbor or trellis. Both the overall style of your landscape and what you want an arbor to convey are important considerations. Functionality is essential, as some structures need to serve a specific purpose, while others are merely decorative. Budget and upkeep should also figure into the decision process.

Ideally, the style of the arbor will harmonize with the architectural style of your home. In addition, take time to consider your design goals. Is the arbor's purpose to announce the entrance to a large formal area or a small intimate one? Will visitors find a rose-filled garden on the other side, or a children's play space? An arbor is a prominent landscape element and generally one of the first things to draw the eye, so choose one that sets the right tone.

To Plant or Not to Plant?

One of the attractive attributes of an arbor is the opportunity it offers for additional growing space, a particularly welcome feature in smaller gardens. However, small delicate arbors are sometimes overwhelmed by densely growing vines and may be more appealing with foundation plants around their base. If you do choose to plant, a sense of proportion is important here as well. Pair delicate vines like clematis and sweet pea with smaller arbors, while saving sturdier vines for large-scale structures.

In addition to shade and fall color, Rogers Red grapes (Vitis californica 'Rogers Red') provide plenty of snacks.

In general, smaller-scale arbors made of lighter materials work for more intimate and informal spaces, while larger arbors are appropriate for larger, more formal ones. Consider shape and detail as well. Arbors with curves and flourishes add classic charm to traditional gardens and informal spaces alike. Functionality also plays a role. If the arbor is over a seating area, protection from the elements is important, and slats with some spacing between them will provide shade and allow any overhead vines to peek through.

Don't forget to take advantage of the vertical growing surfaces arbors provide to sneak in a few edibles. An arbor draped with grapes or kiwis provides beauty, shade, and food, and what could be more stylish than that?

Wood or Metal?

Wood and metal are the most popular materials for arbors. Wood arbors are generally informal and may be painted or stained. For a warm and cozy feel, it's hard to beat the classic combination of a white-painted arbor accenting a rose or cottage garden. Larger arbors made of wood can take on a rustic character, particularly when paired with stone or other heftier materials. In addition to choosing a material based on how effectively it works with your overall design plan, upkeep is also a consideration. Wood arbors need regular maintenance, and will require repainting or restaining, as well as resealing.

Metal structures can adapt to a range of styles. Metal arbors with simple designs and strong geometric lines are ideal for setting off more contemporary gardens, or even traditional gardens with complex planting beds. Their clean, simple design can provide a quiet contrast. Arbors with ornate and curling styles are reminiscent of classic cottage gardens or European-style architecture, and work well both in old-fashioned and traditional surroundings.

An arbor doesn't need to be expensive to have a big impact. Simple, prefabricated arbors of painted wood or aluminum are readily available from online sources or at most garden centers and make a practical choice.

A white arbor is a classic choice for a cottage garden.

The clean lines of this metal trellis are simple yet elegant.

Redefining Trellises

Wood and metal are the default choices for garden structures for good reason—they're affordable, sturdy, readily available, and fit well in a range of landscapes. But if you want to include something with a bit more personality, consider other materials. Unfinished wood or logs make a delightful rustic-style trellis, while bamboo has become increasingly popular due to its good looks and because it can be sustainably harvested.

For the truly adventurous, creating a structure out of living material elevates an arbor or trellis to a work of art. For a showstopping effect, use living branches or reclaimed objects in place of traditional construction materials.

As fond as we are of plants, a trellis can still add amazing vertical interest to a garden despite an absence of greenery. Not only can a trellis double as a work of art in your garden, but it can serve as a focal point that sets off the landscape around it.

Hand-cut branches lend a rustic feel to a garden.

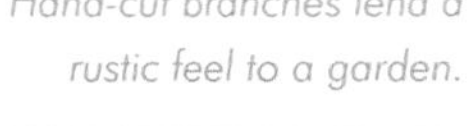

Color

If you're a do-it-yourselfer, you may already know that one of the easiest ways to add a wow factor to a simple wooden trellis is a few coats of paint. This budget-friendly trick can save money—leaving a bigger budget for plant shopping. And what better way to create a signature look in your garden than by choosing a color uniquely your own?

If your goal is simply to keep your trellis tidy and you're not looking to make a statement, consider muted or earth tones. When a trellis is the only thing breaking up a wall of green, it's hard

Repurposed garbage cans and willow cuttings create a trellis that is green in every sense of the word.

*Orange clock vine (*Thunbergia gregorii*) and gloriosa lily (*Gloriosa superba*) twine through a bright purple trellis.*

to go wrong with cobalt blue or purple, as these cooler colors provide contrast without taking over a space. For a more adventurous option that still maintains a sense of harmony, paint a trellis in a shade that's complementary to whatever is blooming close by.

The trellis focuses the view on a charming barn in the distance.

Framing the View

Anchoring a Space

Let's face it; it isn't called the great outdoors for nothing. Spending time outside is such a rewarding experience in part because of the open space and interesting surrounding views. These elements just can't be reproduced indoors. You have several options available to make the most of the views in or around a garden.

Larger gardens or those with expansive views can often feel oversized. Using vertical objects in the foreground to frame views in the background is a favorite designer trick. This is an excellent way to draw attention to a particularly attractive portion of the view, and it also breaks down an overwhelming vista into manageable chunks. Vertical elements in the foreground also help anchor a garden, ensuring that it doesn't get lost in the larger landscape.

In smaller gardens, views are often "borrowed" from surrounding properties. For most of us, the word "view," when applied to landscapes, conjures up pictures of sweeping vistas or distant mountains, but a view can be simple. Focused on our own gardens, we sometimes forget to look beyond the fences that contain them. Look around the garden and see if there are any neighboring views you can emphasize. It could be something as simple as a tree in a nearby yard that provides a scenic backdrop for your own garden, or the charming sight of your neighbor's porch swing, glimpsed through a frame of greenery. Vertical elements in your own garden such as tall and narrow evergreens, arbors, or trellises can act as frames for the surrounding landscape, essentially adding an adjacent garden to your own.

This arbor was specifically built to frame the picturesque neighboring porch.

Framing A View

Framing views, whether within the landscape itself or between a home's interior and the surrounding landscape, is a principle of traditional Japanese garden design, and a simple way to create a harmonious space.

A narrow side-yard fence is turned into a focal point wall to create a charming view from inside.

This narrow kitchen window was added specifically to bring the garden and sweet scent of jasmine inside.

Inside-out Design

The concept of borrowing and framing views can work inside the home as well. As designers, we hate to see any part of a garden wasted. In our experience, side yards often represent untapped garden potential. Even if a side yard is too narrow or out-of-the-way to be easily integrated into the rest of the garden, it can still enhance the inside of your home. Consider the windows of the kitchen, bedroom, or other rooms in the house as a frame, and fill them with views of plants and garden objects to be enjoyed from inside.

Even very narrow side yards with little room for plants can be reinterpreted this way—simply treat a fence as you would a wall inside your home. You'll have a vertical "canvas" ready for whatever you want to add. When it comes to deciding what to plant, the sky's the limit! Choose plants and objects that have meaning for you, or coordinate the plant palette with colors of the room. Bringing the outside in is one of the easiest ways to enjoy your garden year-round.

All gardens have their challenges, and as often as not, gardening up is where the answer lies. A planting bed so narrow there's barely room for

NNY SPACES

one plant, let alone a combination? No privacy from your neighbors? With a little planning and the right plants, even the narrowest plots can be transformed into beautiful garden spaces.

Solutions for Narrow Planting Beds

Layer Up Instead of Out

A lush, colorful perennial border is at the top of most gardeners' wish lists and for good reason. With its lavish mix of flowers and foliage, a well-designed perennial bed never fails to delight. At the heart of any successful border is a skillful layering of height, color, and texture. Believe it or not, even small-space gardeners can achieve this multilayered look. What's the key? Layer *up* instead of out.

The traditional approach to planting a border is to work from back to front, with large shrubs in the rear, medium-sized grasses and perennials in the middle, and low-growing border plants in the front. Narrow spaces simply don't have the room for this. But by creating layers vertically instead of horizontally, even beds a few feet wide can rival the most lavish perennial border.

(Previous page) By layering up instead of out, an ultra-skinny bed becomes home to a wide variety of plants.

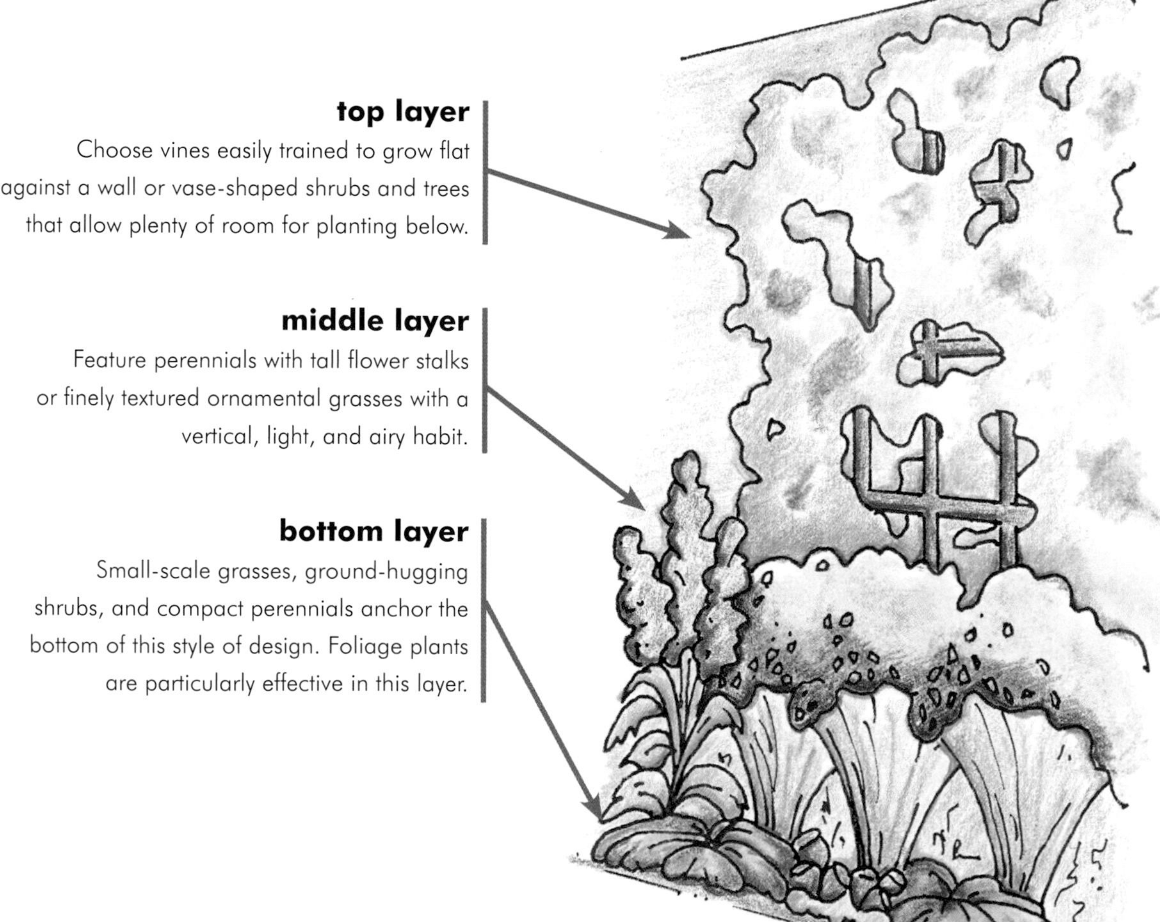

Dramatic seedpods make this clematis a show-stopper in winter.

Sweet autumn clematis is a good choice for narrow spaces.

The top layer is the backbone of a vertical bed. Tall, narrow shrubs, small trees, and vines belong here. Make sure that the branching structure of whatever you plant leaves room for additional layers below. Shrubs or woody vines that can be pruned into a vase shape (full on the top and narrow on the bottom) are ideal. Trees with a slender trunk and arching habit like boxleaf azara (*Azara microphylla*) work well, as do those easily controlled by pruning, such as pineapple guava (*Feijoa sellowiana*).

Plants that develop moderately woody bases over time such as bougainvillea or climbing roses are also good choices, as their flowers arch out to form the top layer of the bed while their bare trunks are hidden by plants in the middle layer. And it's hard to beat the timeless charm of climbing roses. When planted along a fence or other support, larger varieties can be trained to grow horizontally along the top of a border. Available in a rainbow of colors, climbing roses fit easily into just about any garden plan.

Finely textured, herbaceous vines (those that die down at the end of a season) are another good choice. Look for vines that will grow flat against a trellis such as black-eyed Susan vine (*Thunbergia alata*) or clematis. Vines like these can be planted close to the base of the trellis, leaving room for smaller plants in front.

Middle Layer

For the middle layer, choose plants with an open habit to help your bed seem lush and full. Our eyes rely on a variety of cues to perceive depth. When two or three plants are visible in a space that appears to only have room for one, an illusion of depth is created. By choosing plants for the middle layer that can be "seen through," your skinny-space garden will appear larger and fuller than it really is. To achieve this in a classic cottage garden, tall flowering perennials and annuals such as

*The open habit of tobacco plant (*Nicotiana mutabilis*) creates an illusion of depth in this planting bed.*

Dramatic coleus mingles with cannas and 'Firepower' heavenly bamboo (Nandina domestica) in a narrow planting bed.

delphiniums, foxglove, and liatris can be mixed together, ensuring that something is always blooming throughout the growing season. For drought-tolerant gardens, look to long-flowering plants with low water requirements, such as purpletop vervain (*Verbena bonariensis*), lavender (*Lavandula intermedia* 'Provence'), and yarrow (*Achillea filipendulina* 'Coronation Gold').

Ornamental grasses are another option for your bed's middle layer. The finely textured foliage and graceful, upright habit of tall grasses such as feather reed grass (*Calamagrostis acutifolia* 'Overdam') provide welcome contrast to flowering perennials.

Bottom Layer

Mounding plants growing no more than 2 feet tall belong on the bottom layer. While flowers are a wonderful way to bring seasonal interest to skinny spaces, adding plants with attractive foliage will keep your garden exciting throughout multiple seasons. Plants with colorful leaves can be particularly effective at the base of a narrow bed, where they provide balance to the flowers higher up in your vertical garden.

Hens-and-chicks add color and texture to the bottom layer of this border.

Nurseries have responded to gardeners' growing demand for top-performing foliage plants with an ever-increasing selection of new plants prized for their leaf color. Hardy coral bells (*Heuchera* sp.) and annual coleus have been garden staples for years and are now available in colors ranging from the deepest burgundy to the brightest green.

When it comes to choosing flowers for this layer, those with a soft, mounding habit are best. Although many garden centers offer a nice selection of annual flowers, we prefer to rely on perennials. Not only do they flower year after year, but many have foliage that remains evergreen or semievergreen throughout the year. One of our favorites is *Geranium* 'Rozanne', with its long-blooming, bright blue flowers that complement almost any planting plan.

DESIGN SPOTLIGHT

From Junkyard to Garden Tour Standout

Although the rest of the garden was both functional and beautiful, this narrow side yard garden had been pretty much written off by the homeowners. Over the years it had gradually become the final resting place for leftover garden clutter and outgrown children's toys. An invitation to participate in a local garden tour turned out to be the incentive the owners needed to finally tackle this challenging space.

Before: *The original concrete path was both uninviting and too narrow to be practical. The few potted plants were too small to camouflage the oversized storage container and were lost in an accumulation of garden clutter.*

After: The side yard is now one of this garden's highlights.

A burgundy-leafed Japanese maple partially screens the storage shed, and sets off the green and silver plants around it.

A birdbath tucked into the planting bed invites visitors to stroll down the path for a closer look.

Plants with finely textured foliage add a feeling of openness to the space.

The gold colored path is wide enough for comfortable strolling and provides bright contrast for the plants growing on either side. From a functional standpoint, it now easily accommodates wheelbarrows and garbage bins. A subtle curve elevates the pathway from purely utilitarian to a garden experience.

The delicate leaves of variegated kiwi vine won't overwhelm neighboring plants.

Choosing Plants

How many different plants does each layer need? That depends both on your space and the style of garden you prefer. Mixing multiple varieties into each layer can result in a lavish and lovely garden, but it's not necessary. If carefully chosen, just one or two varieties for each layer, repeated as needed, can provide plenty of interest.

Regardless of how many plants you ultimately choose, keep in mind the design principle of repetition. In skinny spaces, the easiest way to accomplish this is to choose one plant for each layer. These three plant varieties will form your base combination. Repeat them at regular intervals and they'll provide the rhythm necessary to keep a narrow bed from becoming chaotic. The following suggestions will help get you started.

If you prefer vines for the top layer, the fine texture of variegated kiwi vine (*Actinidia kolomikta*) works well in narrow spaces. Alternatively, flowering maple (*Abutilon* sp.) is an herbaceous shrub that can be easily trained to grow flat along a wall, and in mild climates will flower year-round.

Options for the middle layer include more compact versions of heavenly bamboo (*Nandina domestica*) such as 'Umpqua Princess', or mountain laurel (*Kalmia latifolia* 'Little Linda'). On the bottom layer, both Scotch heather (*Calluna vulgaris* 'Gold Haze') and dwarf conifer (*Cryptomeria japonica* 'Tansu') are well behaved, compact, and colorful.

Long-Lasting Scent

For scent that lasts beyond one season, plant an old-fashioned sweet pea vine at the base of a scented dwarf climbing rose such as 'Dream Weaver'. The sweet pea will use the canes of the rose as a trellis and perfume your garden in the spring, and as an added bonus make excellent cut flowers. By the time the sweet pea has finished blooming, 'Dream Weaver' will be just getting started filling the air with its spicy apple fragrance.

Flowering maple's (Abutilon megapotamicum 'Halo') dainty, bell-shaped flowers bloom year-round in mild climates.

Regardless of the layer, avoid shrubs that are too dense. Wider shrubs traditionally used for hedging will require constant shearing to maintain the correct width. Not only will forcing a shrub into an artificially narrow space limit your ability to layer other plants into your garden bed, but it will eventually lead to a woody, unhealthy specimen. A plant that has been trained to grow flat against a wall, trellis, or fence is called an espalier. Plants that respond well to being trained as an espalier are an excellent choice for smaller beds. If you lack the time or patience to train a young plant, many garden centers carry popular shrubs, such as camellias or citrus, already espaliered onto a trellis.

Although we've focused mostly on plant form, many plants have traits that will allow you to create a multisensory garden. Even a small-space garden can really make an impact when plants offering scent, touch, and movement are included. For scent, look to vines with fragrant blossoms, such as star jasmine (*Trachelospermum jasminoides*), pink jasmine (*Jasminum polyanthum*), or honeysuckle (*Lonicera* sp.). Softly textured lamb's ears (*Stachys byzantina*) and mullein (*Verbascum thapsus*) invite passersby to stroke their fuzzy leaves. Ornamental grasses with fine, narrow foliage, such as dwarf fountain grass (*Pennisetum alopecuroides* 'Little Bunny') or ruby grass (*Melinis repens*), are ideal for adding movement to your garden, as their delicate leaves sway gently in even the slightest breeze.

Tidy and compact ruby grass waves gently in the wind.

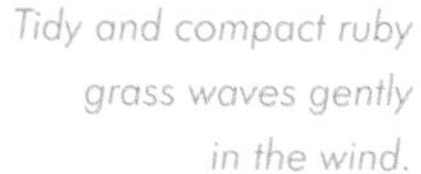

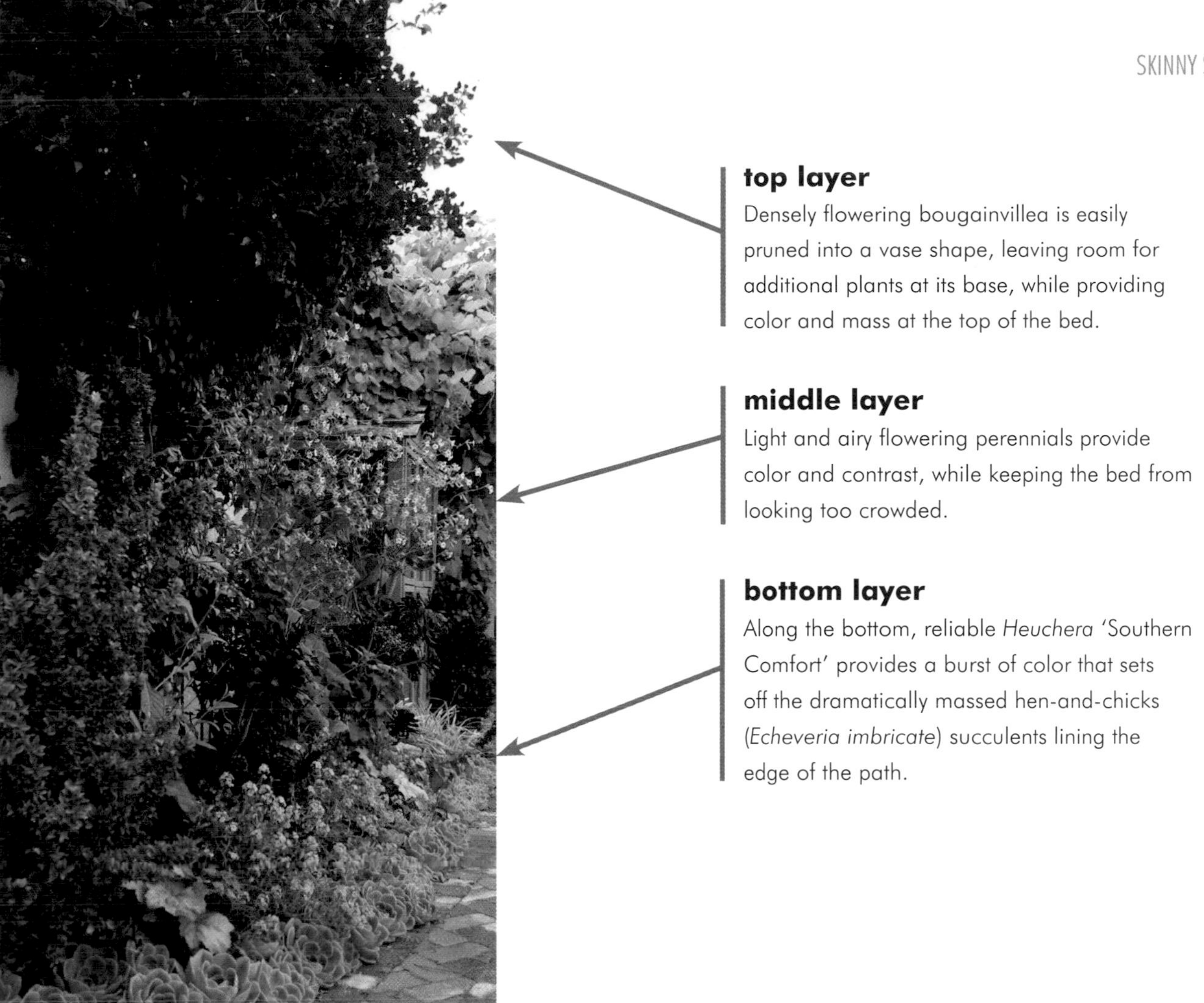

Ultra-Narrow Spaces

Ultra-narrow beds can confound even the most experienced gardeners. To achieve the desired height, a common solution is to choose a large-scale shrub, then shear the life out of it to keep it from encroaching onto nearby paths and patios. Not only is this a ho-hum design solution, but planting a wide shrub in a too-small space means it must be constantly pruned to maintain its shape. Even diligent homeowners will have limited success with this plan, as regular shearing of new growth will ultimately result in a woody, twiggy mess. Additionally, this approach ignores the sustainable gardening principle of "right plant, right place," which encourages gardeners to select plants that don't require constant pruning to maintain their shape, thus reducing the impact of yard waste on local landfills.

But don't despair! It is possible to create a rich and complex planting area in the smallest of spaces. Although the bed pictured above is only 18 inches deep, its multilayered design really packs a punch.

Dramatic horsetail stands out against a gold wall. Highly invasive, this plant should be confined to containers.

Plant Massing

An alternative to layering a skinny-space garden is a mass planting of just one or two plants. This design strategy works particularly well in extremely narrow beds or when a more complicated plant grouping is not desirable. If you prefer a landscape with a contemporary edge, plant massing provides a clean, crisp effect, while still offering a rich, full look. Plants should be spaced to touch, or almost touch, when they're mature. The result will be a flowing, uninterrupted line that is both striking and harmonious.

Plants with an open habit add architectural interest when massed along a fence or wall. We're particularly drawn to perennials with brightly colored blooms that make a dramatic statement against a contrasting background. Tall and colorful kangaroo paw (*Anigozanthos* 'Harmony' or 'Bush Red') blooms on 4- to 6-foot-tall stalks from spring through fall, while taller varieties of red-hot poker (*Kniphofia uvaria* 'Royal Standard') are topped by 4-foot-tall torchlike, lemon yellow flowers. Plants such as horsetail (*Equisetum hyemale*) make such a strong vertical statement that flowers become unnecessary.

Anigozanthos 'Harmony' has prolific 4 to 6 foot spikes of yellow flowers that resemble kangaroo paws.

Red-hot poker sends up brilliant orange "torches" from spring through summer.

The leaves of Canna 'Phaison' capture the light.

Fast growing cannas can be grown as annuals in colder climates.

Canna 'Pretoria' has dazzling orange flowers that bloom all summer long.

When Less Is More

If you prefer a lush look but lack the space to layer effectively, look for plants that combine a mix of color and texture within a single specimen. Hardy to Zone 7, cannas are an excellent choice for massing and are particularly appropriate grouped close to swimming pools or anchoring a tropical planting scheme. Brightly colored flowers in shades of yellow, orange, and salmon provide showy summertime color, but the leaves pack a punch as well. Look for newer varieties, which are prized by gardeners for their variegated leaves that range from the rich bronzy-black patterns of 'Phaison' to the green and gold striping of 'Tropicana Gold'.

Up Against the Wall

Privacy Screening

Many new housing developments are built to maximize indoor living space, with less thought given to how oversized houses on small lots affect outdoor living space. The result is often two-story homes built so closely together that it's easy to feel as if you're living in a fishbowl. If this describes your landscape, then using trees to create a privacy screen may be the best solution, as the height they provide not only blocks views from upstairs windows into your garden, but also creates a greater degree of privacy inside your home.

Identifying trees for this situation can be challenging, as narrow lot dimensions—not to mention homeowners association rules—often restrict how close to the property line trees may be planted. Reviewing a few guidelines before you go tree shopping will ensure that you choose trees that are right for your situation.

Look for columnar shapes. Trees that grow more narrowly can be planted closer to the fence line without infringing on your neighbor's garden or overwhelming your own. Look for trees with a mature width of 6 to 12 feet. While larger trees may be kept to a narrower form with regular pruning, not only can this become a tiresome garden chore (made even more difficult by the need to access your trees from your neighbor's property), but it usually results in an unhappy, unattractive specimen.

The maroon foliage and sizzling red flowers of crape myrtle (Lagerstroemia indica 'Dynamite') make an outstanding combination.

Evergreen Carolina laurel cherry is easily pruned into a small tree shape.

Is year-round screening important to you? If so, your choices will be limited to evergreen trees. While an all-evergreen screen will result in more privacy, banning deciduous trees (those that lose their leaves in cold weather) from your garden eliminates opportunities for multiseason interest. A mix of evergreen and deciduous trees is often a better choice. When determining placement, for most homes the best location for deciduous trees is at the southwest corner of the house. In summer, when the tree is in full leaf, it will block the intense afternoon sun. In winter, its leafless branches will allow the sunshine inside to warm the house.

Think beyond trees and consider shrubs that can be pruned into a tree shape. The majority of trees grow 25 to 40 feet tall. Too many tall trees can quickly overwhelm a smaller garden. Although they are often kept to much smaller heights, many shrubs commonly used for hedges can actually be trained as small trees. Options include mock orange (*Pittosporum tobira* 'Variegata'), Christmas berry (*Photinia fraseri* 'Birmingham'), or Carolina laurel cherry (*Prunus caroliniana*).

With their collection of antique watering cans, Freeland and Sabrina Tanner turned an ordinary, vine-covered fence into a unique, personal expression.

Beyond Green Fences

Keep It Simple

Garden designer Laura Schaub overlays a narrow mirror with a decorative frame to give the illusion of a doorway to another space.

When we first meet with a new client, we are often asked to suggest vines appropriate for covering bare wooden fences. We're all in favor of adding some vertical magic to unadorned garden spaces, but planting a fence with a continuous row of vines often just means you've exchanged a brown fence for a green one. While that's a step in the right direction, instead of regarding a fence as an eyesore that must be hidden at all costs, think of it as a blank canvas just waiting for the right mix of plants and accessories to transform it into an eye-catching addition to the garden.

The backbone of your planting beds will be a mix of vines and shrubs. Delicate vines such as silver lace vine (*Polygonum aubertii*) or fiveleaf akebia (*Akebia quinata* 'Shirobana') have an airy, lacy quality that makes a lovely contrast to more densely leafed plants and allows portions of the fence to peek through. Mixing together more than one species also adds a greater range of seasonal interest to your garden. However, limiting your palette to one specific vine can also be effective, particularly if you plan to add art or other accessories to the mix. Shrubs also work well as a background plant if you choose those that can be espaliered or otherwise trained to grow flat against a fence, such as camellias or holly. Evergreen shrubs are often slower growing and can be easier to control than many vines.

Once a backdrop of vines and espaliered shrubs has been created, use dense shrubs for punctuation rather than planting them all in a row. Upright, narrow shrubs scattered throughout provide appealing contrast to the more open, delicate habit of plants that hug the wall. Some of our favorite choices are pittosporum (*Pittosporum tenuifolium* 'Oliver Twist'), euonymus (*Euonymus japonicus* 'Green Spires'), and dwarf Eastern arborvitae (*Thuja occidentalis* 'Piccolo').

Keep in mind that it isn't necessary to entirely hide the fence. A fence covered in a dense green layer of leaves can be just as overpowering and uninspiring to look at as the original bare wood. Allowing portions to peek through not only provides

Shawna Coronado highlights a garden wall with her grandmother's collection of glass balls and antique insulators.

some contrast, but also leaves space to tuck in accessories. Adding a mirror is a classic technique used by interior designers to reflect light and make a space seem bigger than it is. The same idea works in a garden. In fact, don't be surprised if visitors don't immediately realize they are looking at a mirror! A reflection of a densely planted garden gives the casual viewer the impression of looking through a window to another garden beyond.

Turn a Fence into a Focal Point

As designers and gardeners, we tend to see any open space as an opportunity to tuck in a plant or two, but sometimes restraint is in order. In a garden that's already densely planted, leaving some part of a fence bare to use as a canvas for accessories or art is a wonderful way to turn that portion of the fence into a focal point.

When choosing garden accessories, there are more options than those that can be found at traditional garden centers. Often, the best source of art to adorn your fences is everyday items you may already have, or a collection of objects that's meaningful to you. Displaying items that connect with your past, your interests, or your family is a charming way to make a garden uniquely yours.

Side Yard Makeovers

Untapped Potential

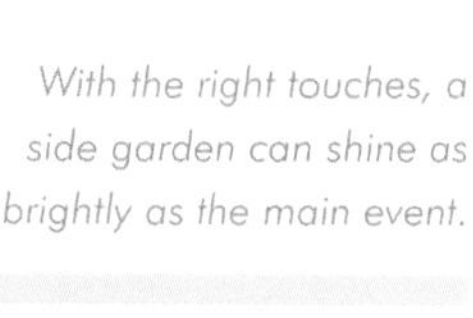

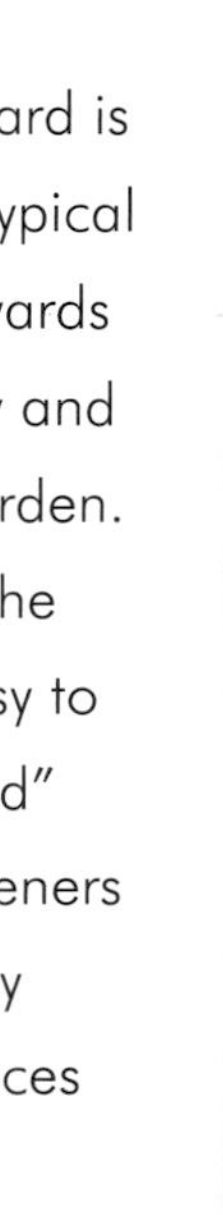

With the right touches, a side garden can shine as brightly as the main event.

For many homeowners, a side yard is merely an afterthought. With a typical width of only 7 to 12 feet, side yards are often considered too narrow and confined an area in which to garden. Since they are hidden away on the side of the house, it's all too easy to take an "out of sight, out of mind" approach. Even dedicated gardeners may find themselves frustrated by the challenges these narrow spaces present, and before long a side yard can become a junkyard—an uninspired space filled with garbage cans, composters, and general clutter.

Side yards, however, can be so much more than that! In fact, we consider them to be prime garden real estate. With a little vertical know-how, these overlooked spaces can be turned into gardens that delight—while still providing space for a trash can or two.

The two most important elements in a side yard are the plants and the pathway. Understanding the characteristics that make a shrub or perennial shine in a narrow garden is the key to choosing the right plants.

Beware of Monster Vines!

Plant tags with words like *fast-growing* and *quick-covering* usually describe vines that grow 20 feet or more. While vines like this can be successfully trained along the top of a fence, they can quickly become thuggish and develop oversized trunks and dense woody growth, traits that are highly undesirable in small-space gardens.

Plant Choices

Plants in narrow spaces need to serve double, or even triple, duty. No one-hit wonders here! Think texture, color, scent, and shape. Choose plants with at least one or more of these features and your garden will reward you with year-round interest.

When planting in cozy spaces, look to plants with foliage that is best appreciated up close, such as threadleaf bluestar (*Amsonia hubrichtii*) or mother fern (*Asplenium viviparum*) with their soft, feathery leaves. In larger landscapes, details like these are often lost, but in tighter quarters the texture of a plant becomes a key attraction.

The delicate texture of mother fern is best admired up close.

Tall plants are essential to turning bare side yard walls into lush gardens, but foliage that is bold or dense can easily overwhelm a small space. Trees and shrubs like Japanese maples, with their delicate, lace-cut leaves, are good choices for narrow side yards, as their airy appearance won't overwhelm the small space.

Gold foliage brightens up a shade garden.

Foliage Color

The narrow dimensions of a typical side yard means it is likely to be in shade at least part of the day. A mix of green, variegated, and chartreuse-colored foliage not only "pops" in a shady garden, but also creates a serene and tranquil atmosphere. Unusual and striking selections to consider include tall, narrow variegated Japanese knotweed (*Fallopia japonica* 'Variegata') or finely textured Japanese forest grass (*Hakonechloa macra* 'Aureola').

Gold foliage is particularly welcome in shady gardens, acting as the missing sunshine to brighten even the darkest corners. Fortunately, there are many varieties of evergreen plants with gold variegated leaves that thrive in the shade, including showstopping Japanese aralia (*Aralia elata* 'Variegata'), small-leafed gold wintercreeper (*Euonymus fortunei* 'Emerald 'n Gold'), or boldly colored silverberry (*Eleagnus pungens* 'Variegata').

Adding burgundy foliage to a garden accomplishes so much: the color cools down the hot tones of an area, creates the illusion of depth through its shadowy tones, separates and highlights other neighboring colors, and leads the eye to specific points of interest. In a sea of green, a splash of burgundy causes the eye to stop in its tracks, allowing a garden to admired at a more leisurely pace.

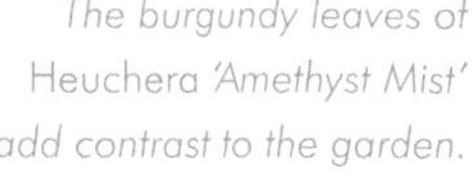

The burgundy leaves of Heuchera 'Amethyst Mist' add contrast to the garden.

Form and Fragrance

The oversized, fragrant blooms on angel's trumpet are available in colors ranging from pale pink to deep yellow to crisp white.

Fragrant plants are a wonderful addition in a side yard garden, as the perfume of even subtly scented flowers is intensified in intimate quarters. Plants that perfume the air include dramatic angel's trumpet (*Brugmansia* sp.), old-fashioned daphne (*Daphne odora* 'Marginata'), or one of the varieties of scented camellias such as 'Scentsation' or 'Scentuous'.

Camellia 'Scentsation' is one of the few fragrant camellias.

When space is limited, plants with tidier dimensions or those that are tall and narrow help soften looming walls without intruding into pathways. When selecting taller anchor plants, consider how you will layer above, around, and below them. Vase-shaped plants are perfect for layering, as are vines that naturally want to hug the fence. Choose denser shrubs with care, as they rarely lend themselves to layering. Instead, select shrubs that have an airy and open appearance. Their lighter feel will be welcome in a closed-in space, and they will be less likely to overwhelm a densely planted bed.

Although their solid structure makes them poor choices for layering, tall, slender conifers and shrubs provide excellent contrast in a narrow border. Plants like *Ilex crenata* 'Sky Pencil' or *Berberis thunbergii* 'Helmond's Pillar' create unexpected exclamation points in your design. Their strong vertical lines are a powerful way to interrupt the horizontal planes of any bed.

The strong vertical shape of an upright holly (Ilex 'Sky Pencil') slices through any horizontal plane, commanding the eye to stop!

Containers

A container nestled within the greenery enlivens this bed, while a strategically placed pot at the end extends the planted space.

Incorporating containers into a planting bed is another way to bring a contrasting vertical element into a narrow space. Containers add much-needed height and help keep plants from overwhelming a pathway. Think beyond simply adding pots to an empty corner. Placing a few containers within a planting bed is an ideal way to liven up a green space.

Be creative in placement. Stack bricks to create a pedestal that elevates a container above the ground, allowing it to attain new status in the garden and become a focal point. If your goal is to give the planting bed a stronger presence, adding pots to the beginning or end will help create the illusion of a much larger space.

Accent on Containers

Keep in mind that containers don't necessarily need to be planted. Unplanted containers, or other garden accessories such as birdbaths or sculptures, not only provide welcome contrast to a planting bed, but entice visitors to venture farther into the garden.

Perfect Pathways

Due to a side yard's constrained dimensions, a common error is to assume that the pathway should be narrow as well. Although it may seem counterintuitive, an artificially constricted path (less than 2½ feet wide) will make your side yard feel more closed in and emphasize its awkward dimensions, while a wider path will give the illusion of a more generous space. On a practical note, side yard pathways need to be wide enough to allow access from front to back and to accommodate wheelbarrows, garbage bins, and foot traffic.

While wider paths will make a cramped space feel more inviting, they also limit the area available for planting beds. When choosing plants, take your time and plan carefully. The layering tips presented earlier in this chapter can help you with your planting plan.

Lush and layered plantings enclose a gently curving pathway.

Incorporating subtle curves is one of the easiest ways to transform a utilitarian side yard into a welcoming garden. Curves add a sense of movement to a space and encourage leisurely strolling. Most important, gentle curves will help break up the bowling alley feel common to many side yards.

Even the loveliest of gardens can harbor an eyesore. Whether it's an ugly (and noisy) air-conditioning unit or a looming utility pole, most of us have something in our gardens that we wish would just go away. When that's not possible,

RDEN SECRETS

vertical garden techniques can help to blend, hide, or soften those offenders. Don't worry; we're not suggesting you reach for a makeup bag—learning a few easy design strategies and knowing the right plants to use is all it takes to make those eyesores disappear.

Blend In

Hide in Plain Sight

While your first thought might be to hide an eyesore with a screening plant, this plan can backfire. Whether a plant stands out or blends in has a lot to do with its texture. A large, dense shrub with big, coarse leaves planted directly in front of an object will often draw the eye toward the very thing you want to disguise. Dense and hulking shrubs tend to visually "swallow" space instead of softly blending in with their surroundings. While it's true that they are effective at blocking a view, they don't provide a particularly attractive option.

From a distance, finely textured plants with small or narrow leaves appeal to the eye without demanding a lot of attention. When disguising something, these are the types of plants to use. Their delicate texture helps an object gently recede into the background when placed in front of, or near, it. The narrow fronds of grasses like *Miscanthus sinensis* 'Morning Light' or the small, variegated leaves and open appearance of shrubs such as *Euonymus japonica* 'Green Spires' are good examples.

(Previous page) Vertical elements transform a tiny suburban garden into a private, tropical retreat.

The narrow, finely cut leaves of Miscanthus sinensis 'Morning Light' make it a perfect screening plant.

Dense leaves create a visual mass, turning a plant into an unintended focal point.

Barbecues and Other Built-ins

To draw attention away from the bulky shape of built-in elements in your yard, such as barbecues, fire pits, or hot tubs, use finely textured plants to help them blend into their surroundings. You won't be able to completely hide these things, nor should you need to, but you can certainly soften their visual impact with a screen of wisely chosen plants.

Keep the plant's ultimate size in mind as you don't want it to grow so large that it eventually overpowers your space. Who wants to be completely isolated from the rest of the yard by a dense, massive shrub when barbecuing or relaxing in the hot tub? Vertical plants work well, as they have the height to get the job done without the density that eats up too much garden space. The plant you choose should also be tough enough to withstand any residual heat or chlorine, such as *Euonymus fortunei* 'Emerald 'n Gold' or *Camellia sasanqua* 'Setsugekka'. And don't forget, plants near barbecues or fire pits can't be allowed to grow too tall or flop over where they might touch a scalding-hot flame or surface—for obvious reasons!

Narrow and tough, Euonymus japonica 'Green Spires' is an ideal choice to disguise a barbeque.

Downspouts

Downspouts are another example of a necessary yet potentially distracting element around your home. Typically made from aluminum, galvanized metal, or plastic, they rarely blend in with the architecture of your house. While they might not be very big, they can be attention grabbers.

Softening the outline of a downspout with larger shrubs is a good way to lessen its impact. Remember, plants with large, bold leaves tend to draw attention. Instead, choose those with soft, feathery foliage, such as yew pine (*Podocarpus microphylla* 'Monmal') or hopseed bush (*Dodonaea viscose*).

Delicate leaves and a form less dense than most shrubs make evergreen hopseed bush an appropriate choice to draw the eye away from the downspout.

There are a few things to keep in mind when selecting plants to place near a downspout. Remember to provide excellent drainage to prevent root rot, especially in wetter climates. And keep in mind a plant's mature size when you plant it so it won't completely block the bottom of the downspout when it's grown.

Some downspouts can be quite beautiful, of course, especially when they are made from copper or another natural material. If you're lucky enough to have one of these, consider growing a delicate vine up the downspout. The beauty of the downspout will still shine through, and the vine will act as another design element.

Mexican flame vine's delicate form allows the beauty of this copper downspout to shine through.

When choosing a vine, make sure it won't grow so large or heavy that it pulls the downspout off the side of your house or covers your roof in a blanket of green. Wisteria, ivy, and trumpet vines, for example, grow too large for a gutter to support. The constant effort required to prevent them from covering a roof makes them an impractical choice. Instead, plant a deciduous vine with an ultimate height of 15 feet. Deciduous vines are lighter, so in stormy conditions are less likely to be pulled off than a heavier, evergreen vine. Examples of delicate deciduous vines to consider are some species of clematis, Mexican flame vine (*Senecio confusus*), and orange clock vine (*Thunbergia gregorii*).

DESIGN SPOTLIGHT

A Touch of Old World Charm

Not only did the oversized chimney dominate this typical suburban backyard, but the space was generally lacking in personality. The challenge: De-emphasize the overpowering chimney, while injecting some much-needed style. A few key plants and accessories are all it took to turn this plain-Jane patio into a European-inspired retreat.

Before: *The homeowners were on the right track when they first attempted to soften the looming chimney by adding plants and accessories. But when a vertical element is as large and colorful as this, a more comprehensive strategy is in order.*

After: *A few small changes can make a big difference.*

Figleaf ivy resists the tendency to become woody over time, and is finely textured enough to allow glimpses of the warm red brick to peek through.

Initially, the fountain was lost against the red brick, but backed by a tracery of green ivy, it's now a focal point while the chimney is transformed into a backdrop.

Details make a difference. The potted topiary balances the scale of the chimney, while antique wrought-iron chairs add a touch of European elegance.

The narrow bed below the chimney leaves little space for layering, but the billowy shape of Geranium 'Biokovo' offers a punch of sophisticated color and helps soften the vertical lines of the ivy-covered chimney.

Hide Away

Out of Sight, Out of Mind

Sometimes something is just too utilitarian or downright ugly to blend in, no matter what. Whether it's an air-conditioning unit, a utility pole, or an unsightly roofline, softening it might not be enough. What you need is a way to permanently hide an object or view, whether that's using evergreen plants, a cleverly placed trellis, the art of distraction, or a combination of all three. When the goal is to completely obscure the view of something, you need to pull out all the stops! With a touch of visual trickery, unsightly eyesores can be permanently hidden away.

A vivid red wall hides unsightly utilities and provides a welcome jolt of color to the garden.

Air-Conditioning Units and Heat Pumps

Why is it that these bulky things often seem to be placed right in the middle of prime garden views? Not only that, but when they're running they are loud, blow off hot air, and add nothing of beauty to your landscape.

When you want to hide an AC or heat pump with plants, choose hardy plant varieties that can stand up to any hot air that will be blowing directly on them. Plants should be spaced a minimum of 2 to 3 feet away from the box, as excellent air circulation is required for the unit to operate efficiently. Also, remember to keep one side of the unit free of any plants for easy access and maintenance.

Avoid the temptation to plant a single specimen directly in front of a heat pump or AC unit; instead of distracting the eye it can have the opposite effect. Placing a group of plants next to the unit will help nudge a viewer's gaze to a more pleasant view.

Because they are the same height and depth, this flowering quince (Chaenomeles) helps an AC unit blend into the planting bed.

Utility Poles

A seemingly simple solution to an unsightly utility pole is to wrap netting around it and grow a vine that will "skirt" the pole. This could be a problem, however, when utility workers need to access the poles. Most utility companies require a 5-foot easement around a pole for access. When plants grow into this space, pruning becomes the responsibility of the homeowner—you. If a plant is not pruned when requested, utility company workers may be forced to prune it themselves, whether the homeowner agrees or not. Though that may not be very often, it's still a possibility, and since the poles are city property, the utility company will always have the right to remove the vines.

Use fast-growing annuals, such as golden hop (Humulus lupulus 'Aureus'), to "skirt" utility poles.

If you choose to plant a vine, make it a fast-growing annual, such as golden hops (*Humulus lupulus* 'Aureus'), black-eyed Susan vine (*Thunbergia alata*), or morning glory (*Ipomea* sp.). Annual vines can grow 20 feet in a single season. If access is required later, removing them is fairly easy and inexpensive.

Utility Boxes

If you have underground utilities, you won't have the problem of looming poles and overhead lines that exists in many neighborhoods. Still, you may end up with a large, unsightly utility box placed on your front lawn. These boxes are typically filled with high-voltage components, so significant open space is required on all sides of the box to allow utility company workers safe and easy access.

A simple solution is to focus on disguising the sides and rear of the box, which are most visible from your garden and home, while leaving the front that faces the street open for easy access.

This can be done by planting flowerbeds to surround the sides and back of the utility box, using a decorative fence or small trellis as the backbone of this small bed. In addition to providing an attractive background for shorter plants, a fence may also prevent plants from spreading into the required open space. Using a trellis to support a small vine creates an additional design layer in the planting beds.

A 'Cecile Brunner' rose adds additional height to a fenceline.

Rooflines

Fast-growing, narrow hopseed bush and compact laurel cherry hide an unattractive roofline.

Love thy neighbor, but not their roofline? In residential neighborhoods, unsightly rooflines are one of the most common complaints heard by garden designers. When choosing screening plants, identifying those that hide an offending eyesore is only half the battle. Instead of dense, oversized shrubs, look for plants that provide additional interest such as scent, bloom, or beautiful, eye-catching foliage.

Climbing roses are a good choice. Depending on the variety, they can fit within a narrow planting bed yet can still grow quite tall, especially when trained along the top of a fence. Climbing roses provide months of gorgeous blooms, a garden full of scent, and decorative rose hips in fall. Even in winter, when the roses have lost their leaves, their bare branches will continue to provide partial screening. Hardy and vigorous climbing rose varieties include 'William Baffin', 'New Dawn', and 'Fourth of July'.

Evergreens are another excellent choice for maximum year-round coverage. When choosing trees and shrubs, those with dense foliage will provide the most privacy, especially in winter. If room allows, place the plants in a staggered pattern rather than in a single straight row; this arrangement increases the area's perceived depth and has more visual appeal. However, in very narrow spaces where only a single row is possible, try mixing the line of evergreens with lower deciduous plants. By staggering heights and mixing your plantings, you not only create beautiful combinations, but you also create an illusion of depth. For more varieties of tall and narrow trees, see pages 188-190 in Plant Picks.

Soften

Take the Edge Off

Why not turn lemons into lemonade? Some objects in your landscape are there to stay. While they might not be the worst offenders, they can still grab more attention than they deserve. If budget or other practical considerations mean they can't be removed, the next best thing is to work with what you have. With a little creativity, you can soften their harsh lines, utilitarian forms, or other unattractive features to minimize their impact while perhaps getting something in return. The right plants, plus materials available at your local home-improvement store or neighborhood garden center, are all you need to soften their look.

A chimney ledge is transformed into a handy shelf for displaying garden art.

Chain-link Fences

Chain-link fences are a fact of life. While they may let you see what lies beyond, more often than not, those views are less than ideal. And it doesn't take a garden designer to see that most chain-link fences lack style as well as prevent privacy. Fortunately, a number of creative and affordable options exist to keep this particular eyesore from grabbing too much attention.

Evergreen in milder climates, dwarf honeysuckle blooms profusely in summer.

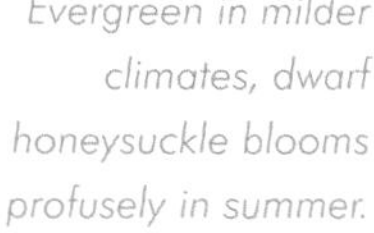

One solution is to use the fence as a giant trellis to support a mix of vines that blends both foliage and flowers. While annual vines grow the fastest, they only last for one season and will need to be replanted each year. For most gardens, perennial or evergreen vines are a better choice as they will provide years of beauty. When choosing a vine, avoid those that develop large and woody trunks. Not only can they overpower a garden, but over time their massive size will destroy a fence. Better alternatives are vines that are manageable in size and weight, such as honeysuckle (*Lonicera* x *brownii* 'Dropmore Scarlet'), evergreen wisteria (*Millettia reticulate*), or silver lace vine (*Fallopia baldschuanica*).

Another simple and inexpensive way to soften your chain-link fence is to install reed fencing. Available at most garden centers, reed fencing is easy to attach to a chain-link fence with twist ties. We love that it offers immediate coverage and provides a beautiful natural background for surrounding planting beds. This type of fencing is available in neutral colors, making it a good choice to create a simple backdrop for lush planting beds. It has the added advantage of providing 100 percent privacy. Depending on the height of your chain-link fence, reed fencing may add to your privacy by providing you with an extra foot or two of height.

Lace vine is a fast growing, semievergreen vine with delicate flowers in spring and summer.

Inexpensive reed fencing provides maximum coverage.

While you might not be able to make your chain-link fence go away, you can turn it into a supporting player by adding an additional layer of fencing. Lightweight wooden trellis panels, easily available from most garden centers, are the perfect choice for this project. Use one of the panels as a template and cut out random pieces to create an interesting geometric pattern. Lay the template over the other panels and repeat the process until you have enough panels to cover the length of the fence. When it comes to choosing a color, the sky's the limit! Choose neutrals if you want the fence to recede into the background, or go bright and bold to create an artistic, one-of-a-kind statement. To take this idea one step further, consider inserting small random mirrors or decorative tiles within the fence.

An artfully cut lattice hides an unsightly chain-link fence and provides a colorful vertical backdrop for the garden.

It's not exactly news that gardens have the power to nurture, soothe, and delight. What is news is the creative approach urban gardeners are bringing to gardening on their balconies and in their courtyards. Today's small-space gardeners are expanding the idea of what a garden can

BAN GARDENS

be, whether that means mixing edibles with ornamentals, creating living wall art, or devising innovative ways to reuse and recycle. Why settle for a few geraniums in a pot when you can take advantage of vertical spaces to create an urban oasis that's uniquely yours?

(Previous page) Bold color and mirrors in the shape of portholes make this focal point wall a dynamic backdrop for a container garden.

A city dweller takes advantage of a fire escape to create a charming container garden.

Benefits of Urban Gardening

The Power of Plants

Ask someone to explain the value of gardening and words like meditative, calming, and creative are sure to arise. Visit just about any public garden and you'll find people of all ages strolling, sitting, or simply being in the moment. Without question, plants can have a powerful impact on our sense of well-being. Fortunately, you don't need a lot of space to tap into these benefits. Urban gardens that take advantage of vertical techniques are popping up everywhere: on balconies, in courtyards—and even on fire escapes!

If you're a city dweller, adding a garden to your courtyard or balcony provides a range of advantages, even if much of your time is spent inside. A lush container garden filters noise and dust, and actually helps cool the air that flows into your home through open windows. Not only that, but a well-planned urban garden provides pleasure by enhancing views from the inside.

A sunny courtyard is home to a vibrant Mediterranean garden.

Urban gardens support butterflies and other pollinators.

The Environmental Connection

Surprisingly, even a small garden in a densely populated urban or semi-urban area can have a positive impact on the environment. As green spaces are paved over to create new communities, concrete, asphalt, and other materials that absorb heat contribute toward a phenomenon known as the heat island effect. In essence, cities become hotter than surrounding rural areas, particularly at night when downtown hardscapes release their stored heat. Plants help to counteract this.

Even in busy metropolitan areas, gardens benefit more than just people. You may not think of a simple container garden as a habitat, but even a small collection of plants plays a role in supporting wildlife. In an urban setting, the distance between open spaces can make it difficult for birds or insects foraging for food to find a place to rest. Planted balconies and courtyards act as rest stops between larger open spaces. This urban wildlife corridor created by city-dwelling gardeners plays an important role in the overall environmental health of a community.

Personal Retreat

Lack of space is often a challenging aspect of apartment or townhouse life. Devoid of greenery, a concrete balcony or a bare, paved-over courtyard doesn't provide much incentive to venture outside. Adding vertical gardening elements with containers, wall planters, or living art is one of the easiest ways to turn an underutilized space into a cherished outdoor room.

Personalizing your space doesn't require a big investment. Setting plants on tables is an easy way to create a multilevel container garden. And remember, benches aren't just for sitting—a rustic flea market find makes a great stand-in for a traditional potting shelf.

An eclectic collection of garden pots adorns a garden fence.

Container Strategies

Layering Techniques

Most small-space gardens simply can't accommodate large planting areas. In traditional planting beds, a mix of tall, medium, and low-growing plants creates depth. While courtyards may include narrow planting beds around the edges, they are just as likely to be completely paved. And, of course, balconies have no planting beds at all. So what's a small-space gardener to do?

To make your space seem larger than it is, use containers to create different layers in your garden. Multiply this effect by including more than one variety of plant within each container. Layering both plants and containers lets you pack a lot into a small space.

In a space less than 3 feet wide, Annie's Annuals nursery layers containers and plants to create a dynamic garden.

A birdcage adds charm to a traditional container garden.

If you're gardening on a balcony, there may only be 1 to 2 feet of space available for containers. Even though your garden lacks the available space to layer outwards, you may be able to layer up. For example, if you already have a collection of smaller pots you wish to use, placing some on plant stands will create a multilevel effect. For maximum depth in very narrow spaces, consider grouping small containers around the base of the stand. The result will be a lush, layered effect.

When placing containers on small balconies, it can be an especially difficult challenge to create the illusion of depth. If all of the containers are the same height and placed close to the wall, the ultimate effect will be two-dimensional. To avoid having your pots look like they're lined up at attention, look for pots in a range of widths and heights to create a dynamic vertical dimension.

We're particularly fond of tall, narrow pots, as they complement the low, wide options that are more commonly found in garden centers. Not only does their smaller footprint make it easier to stagger containers in a tight space, but the taller containers make smaller plants an option as well, increasing the range of plants that can be used to create a vertical effect.

In small spaces, choose plants and containers thoughtfully, as they are likely to be viewed up close. This is not the place for chipped, ordinary containers or spindly plants!

> **Think Outside the Pot**
> A beautiful container can turn everyday plants into a stylish composition. Edibles don't have to be planted in ho-hum glazed pots. Contained in an elegant copper planter, even an ordinary tomato plant becomes extraordinary.

Choosing Containers

The best gardens are personal. While this is true of gardens of any size, the small scale of the typical urban plot means that every container and every plant choice is an opportunity to express your own unique point of view. When we're helping a client create a garden on a larger scale, containers are only one small part of a much bigger set of design considerations. In an urban garden, the containers usually *are* the garden. So why waste time on containers that are ordinary or predictable? Each container should speak for itself.

Before heading to the garden center to choose pots or pick out plants, take some time to think about what inspires you. You might find yourself drawn to certain styles or materials—even something as simple as color can serve as your inspiration.

Cherry tomatoes thrive in an elegant copper planter. Metal conducts heat, so ensure plants stay healthy by monitoring soil moisture if the planter is in a hot exposed site.

A common design suggestion is to create a "family" of containers by choosing pots that share characteristics such as color or style. While we agree with that advice to a point, not every pot you choose has to follow this rule. Mixing in nontraditional planters can soften the effect of a wall full of containers. You don't necessarily need a trip to a garden center or home improvement store—you'd be surprised at how many items you have around the house that can be repurposed into planters.

Three contemporary pots make a graphic statement.

An old toolbox is given new life as a planter.

Of course, not all urban gardens need to be lush and layered. If you favor a more contemporary style, don't be afraid to make a graphic statement with a group of matching plants and pots in a minimalist arrangement.

The Three S's: Soil, Sun, and Size

Soil—Unlike plants in the ground, those in containers cannot send their roots out in all directions searching for food and water. This makes selecting the right soil and fertilizers one of the keys to happy plants. Don't use any old soil for your container; opt for a high-quality organic potting soil. Remember that even the richest growing medium will become depleted of nutrients over time. Slow-release fertilizers will help keep your plants healthy. If you prefer to use organic amendments, consider one of the ready-made compost "tea bags" available on the Internet or from garden centers.

Sun—Lighting often poses a problem for balcony and courtyard gardeners. One side might be intensely bright, while the other side remains in the shade. Understanding how the quantity of light is defined is important. If the tag says a plant requires full sun, make sure it's in a space that receives a minimum of six hours a day in the summer. Part sun is generally defined as four to six hours a day. Plants in pots dry out much faster than those in the ground. Full-sun plants should be watered on a regular schedule during the hottest months.

Prepared compost tea bags are an organic option for maintaining soil health.

A fiberglass pot is a lightweight alternative to heavier materials.

Size—To live happily ever after, plants need room for their roots to grow. If you want larger plants to provide vertical interest or privacy, make sure you choose a larger pot. Take time to determine the exact location before filling the pot with soil, as oversized containers will become too heavy to move easily once they're filled and watered. If weight is an issue, consider pots made from lightweight material such as plastic, fiberglass, or fiber clay, which can mimic the traditional look of terracotta or glazed ceramic at a fraction of the weight.

Make Your Own Shade

In hot climates, unwatered plants in containers can pass the wilting point in as few as twenty-four hours. Take some of the pressure off by planting smaller annuals and perennials under patio trees. The leafy foliage of the specimen tree will help provide dappled shade for tender understory plants.

DESIGN SPOTLIGHT

A New Orleans–Inspired Retreat

On a visit to a garden show in San Francisco, designer Jenny Peterson fell in love with the lush detail of a show garden with a Creole jazz theme. Determined to bring the same eclectic mix of Old World charm, musical inspiration, and romantic plantings to her own Autsin, Texas, balcony garden, she adapted the theme to suit her location. Undeterred by the small space she had to work with, Jenny took advantage of walls, railings, and carefully chosen vertical elements to bring her sumptuous vision to life.

Her Inspiration

Landscape Designer Dawn Engel's The Salvaged Creole Jazz Garden *not only received multiple awards at the San Francisco Flower and Garden Show, it served as inspiration for this romantic balcony garden.*

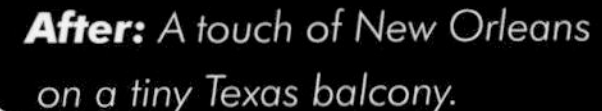

After: *A touch of New Orleans on a tiny Texas balcony.*

In keeping with the musical theme of the garden, a hanging planter resembles the shape of a drum.

The space-saving form of a boxwood topiary makes it an ideal choice for narrow spaces, while its formal appearance recreates the feel of a New Orleans courtyard.

A salvaged trumpet, overflowing with the elegant succulent known as string of pearls, (Senecio rowleyanus) fills a narrow wall.

Even an exposed balcony can feel like a cozy retreat when you bring the indoors out with accessories like patterned rugs and lush throws.

Just about anything can be reinvented as a planter.

A pedestal elevates an old teakettle overflowing with burro's tails (Sedum morganianum).

Reuse and Recycle

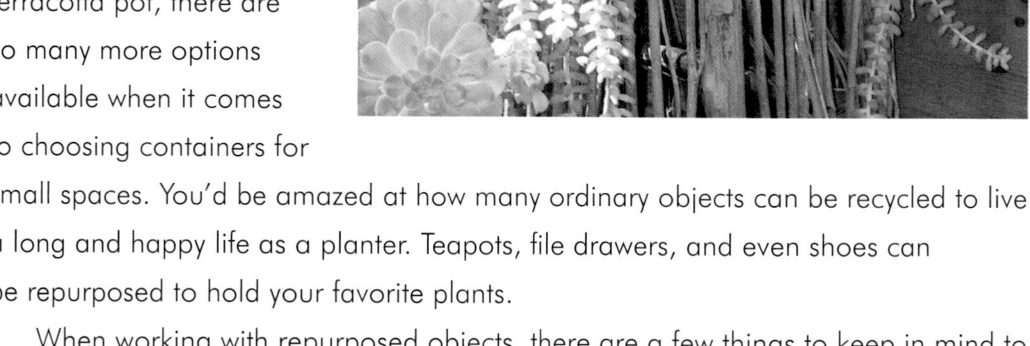

While there's nothing wrong with a sturdy terracotta pot, there are so many more options available when it comes to choosing containers for small spaces. You'd be amazed at how many ordinary objects can be recycled to live a long and happy life as a planter. Teapots, file drawers, and even shoes can be repurposed to hold your favorite plants.

When working with repurposed objects, there are a few things to keep in mind to optimize the health of your plant. Drainage is a crucial component in any container. One of the quickest ways to kill a plant is with soggy soil, which causes root rot. In addition, plants need enough room for their roots to spread and grow. This doesn't mean smaller containers won't work, but in those instances, consider shallow-rooted bedding plants like pansies or calendula, rather than taller perennials that require more root space. And if your garden is exposed to hot sun, avoid small metal containers that are prone to overheating as they'll burn the roots of the plants.

Do It Yourself

Succulent Wall Art

Although kits that include succulents already planted within a frame can be purchased, an alternative is to design and create your own succulent wall art. We used a prefabricated frame available online, but you can also build your own, or even repurpose items like window frames or organizers.

Succulents are ideal for this project; they have a shallow root system that won't outgrow the frame and can go for extended periods with no water. As the succulents grow and flower, the look of your wall will change. Not only that, but each succulent is self-contained in a cozy bundle, making the plants easy to rearrange into different and varied designs. And isn't that the very definition of a living wall?

Succulents are included with this kit, making it easy to create a beautiful piece of living art.

Steps for Success

Step 1. Gather Your Tools

- A frame, either purchased, recycled, or constructed. If using something that won't easily hold the succulent bundles, you may need to affix a mesh screen to the back. The closer the holes in the mesh, the more tightly packed your succulents can be.
- Mounting hardware appropriate for the type of wall or fence you'll be using.
- Succulents, either purchased or garden cuttings
- Sheet moss and cactus mix
- Heavy-gauge scissors
- Floral wire, plastic coated so it won't rust
- Screen material

Simple tools are all that's required for this project.

Sheet moss holds the soil in place.

Step 2. Bundle the Succulents

Cut circles of screening material approximately 10- to 12-inches. The diameter of the circle will vary depending on the succulent size.

Lay some sheet moss on the screen to hold in the soil and put a small amount of soil on top. Place the succulent in the center of the screen, loosening its roots if necessary.

Bundle the roots, moss, and soil with the screen, securely tying it together with floral wire as close to the neck of the succulent as possible.

Create Your Design

Move your bundles around until you find a combination that you like. If the succulents will be tightly packed, mimic the design techniques used for large-scale walls and arrange the succulents to create miniature waves of color and texture. To complement the contemporary look of the frame in this example, we've chosen an open, minimalist design, and simply scattered a few select bundles across the frame.

Cool blue hens-and-chicks form a wave that connects the two frames.

Maintain Your Creation

Because the bundles are exposed on all sides, the succulents will dry out faster than if they're planted in the ground or in a container, so a location in part sun is ideal. You'll need to experiment to determine the right amount of water for its location. A good place to start is to mist with a hose once a week in warm weather and once every few weeks when the temperatures drop. Alternatively, you can deep soak the bundles for thirty minutes at a time, allowing them to dry thoroughly between soakings. In most parts of the country, winter months are too cold to maintain a succulent wall outside. Your wall art can be overwintered in a greenhouse or even used to decorate a sunny interior wall.

Balcony Basics

Maximizing Space

We could trot out a cliché like "Good things come in small packages," but the truth is, if you garden on a balcony, finding enough room for plants takes some ingenuity. Once you've used up all the floor and table space available, the next logical step is to think vertically.

Using the walls of the building is an easy way to carve out additional space. (See chapter 5, "Edibles," and chapter 6, "Living Walls," for a range of growing options appropriate for apartment dwellers.) A vertical garden attached to an apartment wall requires careful planning. Remember that the weight of the planters will increase when the soil is wet and as the plants grow larger. A planting scheme that is too ambitious could result in a hanging garden too heavy for the wall to support.

Although made from lightweight resin, this fountain was too heavy to hang on the wall so a false wall was built to support it.

If your plans include something even heavier and more permanent, such as a fountain, be sure the walls can handle the weight. Otherwise, you may need to construct a false wall and paint it to match the permanent wall.

Herbs are a natural choice for a sunny spot.

Of course, not all leases allow renters to attach objects to the walls. An alternative is to create a garden that attaches to the railings of a balcony. Because a balcony's edges are likely to receive the most direct sunlight, a garden on rails is a particularly good choice for growing cooking herbs, lettuces, or sun-loving annuals. Even if your railing is wide, it's not safe to simply set the pots on top. Make sure they are securely fastened, as wind or other movement can send your container garden tumbling over the side. A typical garden center will have a selection of hanging planter styles to choose from. Alternatively, opt for containers that simplify the process by easily conforming to odd-shaped rails without the need for special fasteners.

While hanging planters are ideal for growing edibles or flowers, for a different effect, consider treating the railing as a trellis and weave a flowering or edible vine throughout its sturdy form.

Wisteria weaves through the railings.

Juliet Balconies

This slender balcony is home to an overflowing garden.

Named for Shakespeare's famous scene where Juliet steps out onto her balcony to hear Romeo's passionate vow of love, we can't resist these romantic, wrought-iron balconies that adorn many city apartments. Often considered too narrow for any type of seating or garden, apartment dwellers frequently treat these tiny treasures as mere architectural details. If you think vertically, however, this underutilized space can pack in more flowers or vegetables than you might expect.

Creating a living wall is a particularly effective solution when floor space is limited to less than a foot or two. The biggest challenge is likely to be the amount of sunlight. If your building is north facing, has a significant overhang, or is in the shade of a nearby structure, the amount of sun it receives may be severely restricted. Conversely, south- or west-facing walls may end up in direct sunlight for most of the day. Before beginning, determine how much sun your garden will receive and choose plants accordingly. Full-sun plants require a minimum of six hours of direct sun a day. Part-sun plants will do well with four to six, and shade plants like less than four.

> **Protect Tender Foliage**
> If you have your heart set on plants whose foliage may be damaged by strong winds, place them in containers lower to the ground. Place smaller plants where they will receive some screening from larger ones.

Coping with Wind

Even balconies only a few floors off the ground are affected by strong winds. Not only does this make it less pleasant to spend time outside, but it also means that plants are more likely to be exposed to damaging winds, resulting in torn and battered leaves. Plants in the *Euonymus, Pittosporum, Phormium*, and *Camellia* families tend to have thick, tough leaves that are less likely to tear in windy conditions. Wind also causes soil to dry out faster, so you'll need to water your plants more often. Even worse, if your pots are not stable enough, they might topple over. Specific environmental conditions, such as salt in the air if you live near an ocean, or snowfall in colder climates, should also be considered when placing containers and choosing plants.

If wind is a major issue, the best defense is heavier pots that resist being blown over. Avoid layering tall plants into balcony containers, particularly herbaceous ones with weaker stems or large, tropical leaves that are easily ripped. As an alternative, consider living wall options that can be attached securely to the wall. For more information on living walls, see chapter 6.

Pots on a railing should always be secured.

Courtyard Style

Bringing the Indoors Out

If you're fortunate enough to have a courtyard, don't think of it as a separate space. Instead, treat it as an extension of your home. In large gardens, designers employ all sorts of tricks to make an expansive space feel intimate. But with its small scale, a courtyard already has the proportions of a room, making the task much easier. And there's no need to create the illusion of walls—you've got the real thing!

An unused courtyard is transformed into a garden retreat.

The more attractive your courtyard is, the more likely you will be to spend time there. The same things that make an indoor room appealing apply outside as well. Comfort is key. While small wrought-iron benches might look picturesque, anyone who has spent time sitting on one knows just how uncomfortable they quickly become. Larger-sized benches and comfortable chairs—even recliners—invite visitors to stay and relax. Pay attention to the arrangement as well; ideally, furniture should be grouped to promote conversation. Adding occasional tables creates space for accessories and also reinforces the idea that your courtyard is not simply an area to pass through, but a room to be enjoyed.

Courtyards might take their cue from the indoors, but don't add too many accessories at the expense of plants. The most welcoming courtyards create the illusion of a private room carved out of a garden. To help create this effect, use containers to tuck greenery behind and around furniture, and take advantage of any surrounding walls. Think of the walls as your canvas to blend elements of interior design with traditional garden touches, such as hanging artwork, lighting, or living walls.

Artistic touches like this garden plaque help turn an outdoor space into a garden room.

An elegant vertical corner planter softens the walls of this courtyard seating area.

Baylor Chapman of Lila B. Designs tucks succulents into repurposed shutters for a dramatic, contemporary effect.

Creating a Focal Point Wall

Courtyards can encompass a range of styles, from traditional to contemporary to playful. Introducing a focal point wall is one way to communicate the style that best describes your courtyard. Typically, this style will be a reflection of the architecture or materials that already exist in the space, but don't be afraid to create a look based entirely on your own vision of what you want it to be.

Choosing one bold element to fill a wall is an effective way to make a statement. This design choice is particularly appropriate for contemporary gardens. A living wall or oversized pieces of artwork are two options to consider. Another approach is to create an accent wall by painting one wall in a unique color. Regardless of your garden's style, when creating a focal point, paint is a inexpensive and easy way to breathe new life into your garden.

The bold color of this wall makes a striking backdrop for plants and containers.

This narrow garden fence combines many of the elements we love to see on a courtyard wall.

Adding a focal point wall is an excellent design strategy for traditional courtyards. Rather than making a dramatic statement with one bold element, a quieter combination of plants and accessories communicates understated elegance. While a contemporary courtyard might play with the notion of what a garden is, for a traditional look, keep the emphasis on the plants. A muted color palette that relies on a mix of green and variegated foliage adds low-key charm, while choosing lighter-density plants keeps a focal point wall from encroaching into the space and allows room for simple accessories.

But simple doesn't mean boring! Combine a few spots of color with traditional accessories such as urns, pedestals, and decorative tiles for a retreat that's restful and serene, yet detailed enough to invite a closer look.

Edibles for Courtyards

For those who garden in small courtyards, growing edibles may seem like an impossible goal. With a thoughtful design and appropriate plants, however, a courtyard can be the perfect place for a vegetable garden.

Because most vegetables become unruly by the end of growing season, courtyard gardeners may hesitate to include them. To avoid this, choose dwarf varieties like bush beans, '8-Ball' zucchini, or 'Window Box' tomatoes. Edibles like these will remain tidy and manageable all season.

If your courtyard has uneven lighting, don't let that discourage you from growing vegetables. Some edibles simply won't produce well without full sun, but many varieties actually thrive in these conditions, including lettuces, onions, spinach, and leeks.

Once they've been harvested, vegetables leave gaps in the garden that are particularly noticeable in small spaces. To carry your courtyard through the winter months, it's important to include evergreen plants throughout your bed. In milder climates, garden sage, blueberries, and dwarf citrus hold their color year-round. In colder climates, consider adding a few nonedible, ground-hugging plants such as *Abelia* x *grandiflora* 'Kaleidescope' or *Pittosporum tobira* 'Creme de Menthe'.

We've said it before and we'll say it again: when designing in small spaces, every element counts. Vegetable beds are no exception. While it's common practice to build traditional raised beds out of wood, an alternative we love is stone. A thoughtfully designed stone bed looks beautiful on its own, even after vegetables have been harvested.

Made from stacked stones, a decorative courtyard vegetable bed provides year-round structure.

Compact '8-Ball' zucchini won't overpower its neighbors.

Stones with angular cuts are ideal for stacking and allow for taller raised beds. However, if your bed will be less than 2 feet tall, rounder stones can be used. Adding a raised bed in such a small space creates an additional level and introduces a welcome change of height.

Trellises are another easy way to bring height and interest to a courtyard. Just as using stacked stone can turn an ordinary vegetable bed into a design feature, decorative trellises in wrought iron or copper add an elegant touch to climbing peas or beans. Even bare, a stylish trellis will continue to look beautiful through the winter months.

Decorative wrought-iron trellises add year-round beauty to climbing edibles.

Once upon a time, having a vegetable garden meant a collection of raised beds, or a few tomato plants in a pot. Instead of being banished to out-of-the-way areas, these days edibles are everywhere in the garden—mixed with ornamentals, scrambling out of recycled containers, and clambering up apartment walls.

EDIBLES

A new range of vertical gardening techniques, from prefabricated hanging planters to repurposed PVC pipe, means even the tiniest garden has room for edible plants. Moreover, even large-space gardeners are reinterpreting traditional vegetable beds and growing their fruits and vegetables vertically. Whether you're looking for ways to grow more in less space or dream of a garden that's as creative as it is functional, there's a *Garden Up!* solution for you.

(Previous page) A few feet of wall surface in a sunny location are all that you need for a vegetable garden.

Edible grapes replace traditional ornamental vines, increasing this garden's harvest.

The Edible Revolution

Why Garden Up?

There's a revolution going on in edible gardening. Once upon a time, only truly dedicated gardeners with room to spare considered it worthwhile to invest in more than a few tomato plants or an herb or two. But all that's changing as more of us realize the nutritional and flavor benefits of growing our own fruits and vegetables. Not only that, but one of the best and easiest ways to ensure that your food is sustainably harvested and safe to eat is to grow it yourself. For small-space or apartment dwellers interested in edibles, gardening up may be the only option. Reinterpreting the classic 4- x 6-inch raised bed into a 5-foot-tall vertical hanging garden, for example, is a creative and practical solution that combines food, gardening, and art. Simply put, growing vertically lets you grow more with less.

Along with rethinking why we're choosing to grow our own food, we're redefining how. Vegetable gardens and fruit orchards were once seen as utilitarian forms of gardening, relegated to the status of trash cans or compost bins and hidden away in a corner. Now, not only do we appreciate the joys of growing our own food, but we also see the beauty of pole beans twining up a trellis or strawberries cascading over the rim of a pot. Gardeners have discovered that edibles belong just about anywhere, whether bursting out of a living wall of plants or tucked among ornamental flower beds.

Vertical gardens fit right into this revolution. As we look to grow edibles in new places and in new ways, vertical techniques are introducing the joys of homegrown food to a whole new generation of gardeners.

Nothing tastes better than a freshly picked tomato warmed by the sun.

Edible Container Basics

Planting Tips

Begin with an organic potting soil that's heavy enough to keep the container from drying out too quickly. When summer temperatures soar, plants can quickly wilt if the growing medium is unable to adequately hold moisture. Keeping an inch or two of mulch at the top of the container will help keep containers moist and your plants healthy.

Edibles are heavy feeders and even a high-quality potting soil lacks all the nutrients they need to thrive. Expect to fertilize regularly. Depending on how often you water, consider applying liquid fertilizer at one-fourth of the rate recommended by the manufacturer with each watering.

If you garden on a balcony or courtyard, your containers might not receive enough sun for the vegetables on your wish list. Full-sun crops like tomatoes, squash, and beans generally require a minimum of six hours of sunlight a day. Fortunately for shadier gardens, there are plenty of edibles that thrive in partial sun, typically defined as a minimum of four hours per day. Some examples are lettuces, spinach, cabbage, leeks, or lingonberries, which have the additional benefit of being evergreen. However, if you live in an extremely hot climate, even full-sun vegetables will appreciate partial shade.

Containers can dry out quickly on hot, summer days. Make sure yours stay well wattered.

This heirloom cauliflower is as pretty as any flower!

The Right Container

When planting in pots, keep in mind the ultimate size of the plant. Many squashes, cucumbers, and other vining plants will quickly outgrow their assigned space and overwhelm a container. This can be a concern even in large gardens; you don't want a pumpkin terrorizing the vegetable patch! Consider varieties that are compact enough for even the tiniest balcony, such as 'Bush Pickle' cucumber, 'Ivory' white eggplant, 'Saffron' yellow squash, 'Gold Rush' zucchini, and 'Sweet-n-Neat Cherry Red' or 'Window Box' tomatoes. Not only will smaller varieties thrive better in containers than their larger counterparts, but you'll also be able to grow a wider selection of edibles.

Prized by gardeners for their sunny yellow color and chefs for their versatility in the kitchen, squash blossoms are a welcome addition to an edible garden.

Crowding plants for visual effect may work when growing ornamentals, but vegetables require sufficient root space to thrive, making crowding them a bad idea. In addition to the size of the plant, you must consider the size of its root system. Yields will be greater if the roots have ample room to grow. Crops like spinach, beans, and eggplant can manage in a 12-inch container, but others like melons and leeks need a container in the 3- to 5-gallon range. If you're planting in hanging "pockets," fast-growing crops with shallow root systems work best, including most lettuces and herbs.

When mixing edibles within an existing ornamental bed, make sure all the plants' food and water requirements are similar. If this is impractical, one option is to put edibles in containers and set them into the planting bed, making it easier to apply extra water. If your ornamental bed has low-water use plants, herbs such as rosemary, thyme, and sage, are reasonably drought tolerant once established and will mix in well.

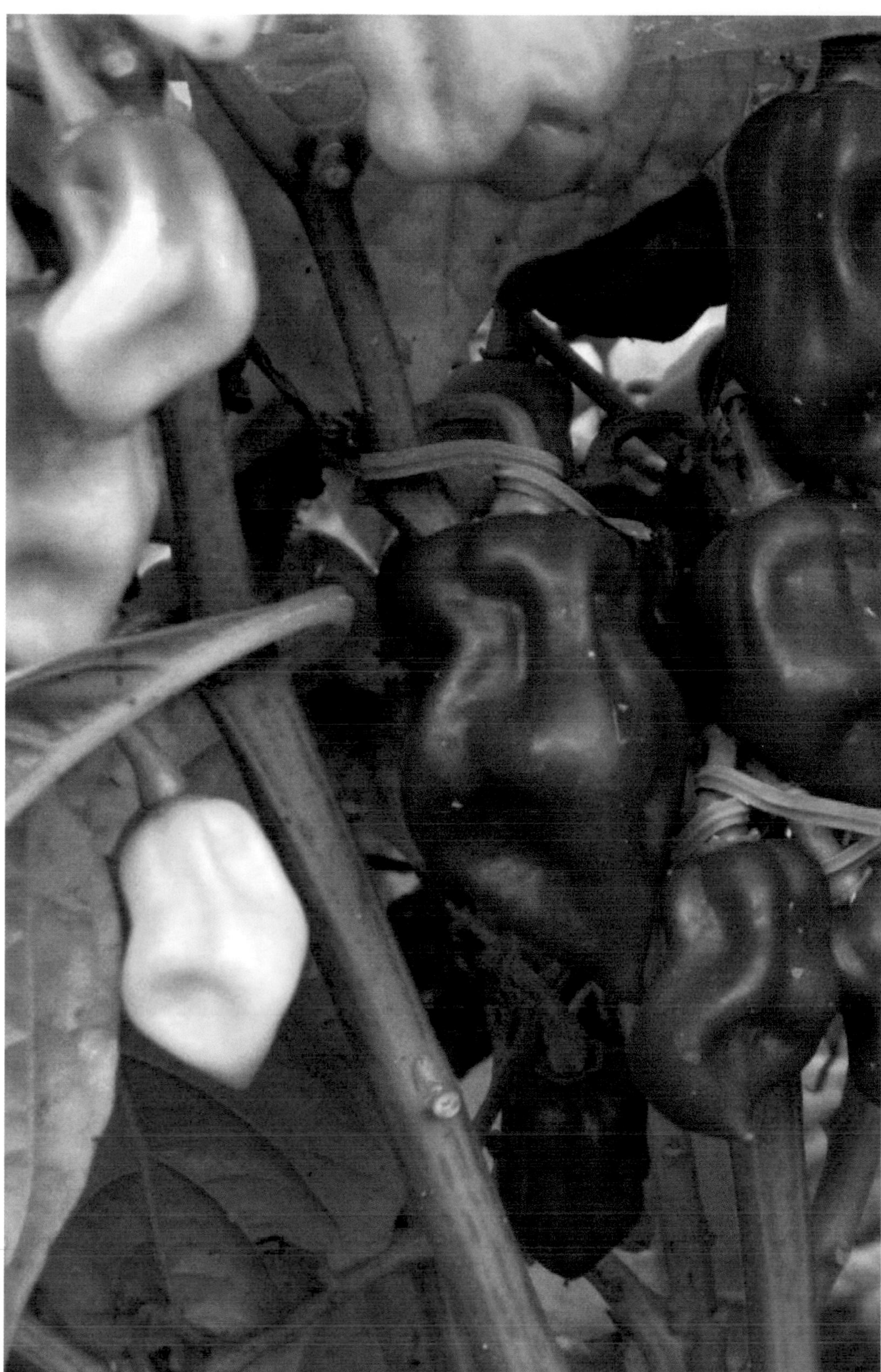

With fruit that ripens to firecracker shades of orange and red, peppers brighten any container.

Climbing the Walls

When Up Is the Only Option

Small cherry tomatoes are ideal to grow on a vertical frame.

When a balcony or patio is dedicated strictly to growing edibles, every inch counts! For plants that normally require a lot of space, gardening up is probably the only option. Fortunately, ramblers such as strawberries, or sprawlers such as tomatoes, are just as happy spreading up as out. The sky's the limit once you begin realizing your space's vertical potential.

Growing vertically has practical benefits as well. In addition to providing the room small-space gardeners would otherwise lack, growing edibles off the ground often simplifies pest management. Many of the most destructive bugs, such as pincher bugs, snails, slugs, and sow bugs, have a much harder time attacking edibles when they have to crawl up a wall or other vertical surface. And don't we all want to make it as difficult as possible for these creepy crawlies to damage our plants?

(Facing page) Pocket systems can hang just about anywhere—even on stair railings.

Hanging Wall Options

Interest in growing food in small spaces has led manufacturers to create a whole range of new products for growing edibles vertically. These units are the perfect solution for creating gardens on balconies or in courtyards where traditional gardening space simply doesn't exist. Hanging wall units also allow those who can no longer get down on their knees to garden, or those who are wheelchair bound, to enjoy the benefits of growing their own food.

Products come in a range of sizes and materials, allowing them to work in a variety of situations. Stand-alone units allow for ease of transportation to sunnier spots throughout the day. Pocket systems that are soft and malleable are ideal for overlapping and for covering corners or large spaces. We also like hanging wall planters made from geometric plastic grids; their simple design allows you to easily interlock multiple panels and attach them to walls.

Drainage and Irrigation for Hanging Wall Units

Before choosing a hanging wall unit, be realistic about how much time and attention you can devote to care and maintenance. Most edibles need to be watered daily during the summer. Unlike traditional plants in the ground that can survive several days between waterings, plants tucked into a typical wall unit's shallow soil pockets will dry out fast. A day or two of neglect can be enough to wilt your entire crop. Fortunately, many units have built-in irrigation systems making regular watering easy to manage.

You'll also need to take drainage into account. All units need to have a way to get rid of excess water. The breathable fabric of pocket-style systems units allows some of the moisture to dissipate, but excess water will still drip through the bottom. While some have built-in moisture barriers to protect walls and furniture from water, most do not. Make sure to choose a location where water damage is not a concern.

A modular wall unit allows you to plant in the narrowest spaces.

Soil and Plants

Soil and feeding requirements for hanging gardens are similar to those of traditional containers. Select a high-quality organic potting soil that provides nutrition and promotes water retention and drainage. Remember that edibles are heavy feeders, requiring weekly applications of fertilizer, so every square inch of soil needs to provide maximum benefits. The soil needs to be loose enough to provide aeration and dense enough to retain moisture. Most high-quality potting soils have these characteristics.

It's also important to choose the right edibles

to match the growing system. Because of the small size of their cells, flat hanging wall units can only support plants with shallow root systems and soft, pliable stems; avoid plants that become large and woody. Good choices are lettuces, strawberries, compact-sized cherry tomatoes, and smaller herbs such as thyme, parsley, and oregano. With their deeper spaces for soil, pocket wall units will accommodate vegetables with larger root systems such as carrots, eggplants, and larger herbs like dill or tarragon.

Whether you choose a grid system or soft-pocket system, vertical options that attach to the wall are best for gardeners who have very limited floor space, can closely monitor irrigation, and want their vegetables to be decorative as well as delicious. For more detailed information on various living wall systems, refer to chapter 6.

Strawberries and herbs adorn a sunny wall.

Sub-Irrigated Planters

Sub-irrigated planters (SIPs) are containers that have a built-in water reservoir under the planter that provides both a steady amount of moisture and a barrier between the roots and the standing water to prevent root rot. SIPs not only simplify regular watering, but require much less water than both ordinary containers and in-ground vegetable beds. The excess water in ordinary containers drains out the bottom and is wasted. The SIP reservoir, on the other hand, contains this excess water. Through capillary action, plants slowly absorb this excess water as needed.

These freestanding types of containers are ideal for growing edibles in small spaces. Unlike vegetable gardens hung on the wall, planters like these have plenty of soil, making it possible to grow a wide range of vegetables.

Because it's simple to attach a trellis or frame, edibles that require support such as beans, peas, or cucumbers can be grown with a system like this. In fact, several planters grouped together are all you need to create an entire vegetable garden.

Edibles thrive in SIPs where their thirsty roots have access to a steady source of water.

Their built-in irrigation systems give SIPs a clear advantage over traditional container gardens, but that's not their only advantage. Once filled with soil, a traditional container can be quite a production to move. In contrast, the SIPs' wheels make moving them to a sunnier spot a snap. In fact, they're so easy to move, you may want to wheel your container to a prime location, where it can take center stage while looking its best. After your crop has been harvested, simply move it discreetly out of the way.

Thanks to this homemade SIP, an underused side yard now has space for a thriving vegetable garden.

If you're the handy type and want more flexibility in size, consider building your own SIP system—but don't forget to include a built-in water reservoir.

SIP systems are best for gardeners who want to maximize the variety of vegetables they can grow, can't manage daily hand-watering, and want a mobile system.

DESIGN SPOTLIGHT

An Urban Homestead

Urban homesteaders are modern-day pioneers who strive to live a low-impact, self-sufficient lifestyle, whether on a quiet suburban cul-de-sac or in the heart of a big city. Gardener Theresa Loe has been practicing sustainable gardening techniques on her suburban plot for years. By taking advantage of the vertical spaces in her tiny walled garden, Theresa has not only increased her harvest, but created a welcoming space filled with whimsical touches.

The Tenants

Charlotte, a Golden Laced Polish, is one of three chickens residing in the tricked out chicken coop that sits at the heart of this charming vegetable garden.

Playful touches like this sign give Theresa's garden a personal touch.

Although much of the vertical spaces are given over to food production, there is room for recycled wall art.

Bean varieties such as scarlet runner bean are a perfect choice for narrow spaces.

To a determined gardener, any surface is an opportunity to plant—even the roof of a chicken coop!

Gutter Gardens

As interest in vertical gardening grows, some of the most exciting innovations are coming from gardeners themselves. People are experimenting with all sorts of systems to make the most of the space that they have. Gutter gardens are popping up everywhere as a creative and ergonomic way to have a vegetable garden in the narrowest of spaces. Whether mounted onto a wall or hanging from an arbor, these planters take vertical gardening to an entirely new level.

Although we're in favor of using recycled materials whenever possible, recycling an older gutter isn't advised for a project like this. Old gutters are usually riddled with rust, which is detrimental to the health of your garden. Not only does rust inhibit growth, but it can also contaminate your produce—and ultimately contaminate you. Use caution with plastic gutters as well, as they're typically coated with lead paint. In addition, plastic gutters break down faster than those made of metal, as they are more easily damage by the sun and by the weight of the gutter once it's filled with soil and plants.

Choose Copper

It's best to use a gutter made of a metal that doesn't rust, such as copper, zinc, or stainless steel. With occasional cleaning and polishing, stainless steel will retain its bright, shiny appearance. Over time, zinc and copper gutters will naturally form a patina in beautiful shades of gray, brown, and green.

Copper may be the best material for gutters. One of the longest-lasting metals, copper is durable and is considered a "green" building material. In addition, the EPA has determined that copper has antimicrobial, germicidal, antibacterial, and fungicidal properties. And that beats a rusty old gutter any day!

Most gutters come in one of three shapes: box, K-style, or half-round. A box gutter is exactly that—box shaped, which means it provides the most volume for soil and plantings. The most common style available is the K-style. It is also boxy, but somewhat angled, which gives it a more stylish look. A half-round gutter looks like a pipe cut in half, and has an elegant appearance.

A gutter garden holds lettuce that can be harvested through a long growing season.

The next step after you've chosen your gutter is to prep it for planting. Drill evenly spaced drainage holes in the bottom of the gutter, and line the holes with

A PVC gutter, end caps and a simple cable trellis system simplify the construction of a gutter garden.

screening to prevent the soil from escaping with each watering. The gutter can either be mounted directly on a fence or wall, or hung with screw hooks from a porch or patio cover for a freestanding hanging garden.

The gutter will become quite heavy once it's filled with wet soil and plants. To ensure that it doesn't collapse under its own weight, it's best to keep the gutter gardens under 6 feet in length. You can also add a mixture of perlite or vermiculite with your potting soil in a one to four ratio not only to help with your soil's aeration, but to reduce the overall weight of the planted gutter. You can also add chicken manure.

The next step is to consider how you'll water your gutter garden. Remember that since the depth of the soil is so shallow, the gutter will dry out much faster than traditional containers. To avoid having to hand-water this garden daily in warmer weather, consider installing an irrigation system with either a soaker hose or individual emitters.

When planting your gutter, refer to pages 86-87 for basic planting suggestions. Edibles that will thrive in a gutter garden are those that have a shallow root system and soft pliable stems, such as lettuces, kale, radishes, cabbages, and herbs. Don't forget to include a few edibles that will beautifully cascade over the side of your gutter, such as strawberries, nasturtiums, and thyme.

Gutter gardens are ideal for the DIY type who is interested in shallow-rooted crops such as lettuces and herbs and who appreciate cutting-edge solutions.

Shallow-rooted lettuces and herbs thrive in this gutter garden.

Pairing Edibles and Ornamentals

Design a Year-Round Garden

An easy way to incorporate more edibles into your garden is to mix them into existing planting beds, where they can mingle happily with their ornamental and evergreen neighbors. Of course, if you mainly grow warm-season vegetables, your lush summer beds will be filled with gaping holes come winter. One way to keep your garden attractive all season long is to mix in evergreens. While that large artichoke with its highly structural leaves and huge purple flowers may look stunning in spring and summer, by winter it will have died back to the ground, leaving a noticeable gap in your planting bed.

To counter this, surround edibles with evergreens, which provide year-round interest in the form of structure or foliage. For example, near an artichoke, try planting small and mounding dwarf forms of Hinoki false cypress *(Chamaecyparis obtusa)* such as "Nana lutea' or 'Pygmaea', or an edible and evergreen lingonberry.

Roses and cherry tomatoes mingle happily together.

Another option that keeps your garden green and growing year-round and maximizes your harvest is to plant edibles in succession. This works particularly well with plants that have a short growing season; as soon as they're harvested, they can be quickly replaced by a different crop.

Vertically trained peas make an excellent spring crop.

An example of this type of succession planting is growing peas in spring, eggplant in summer, and kale in fall. Or try spinach in spring, cucumbers in summer, and cabbage in fall.

Planted when spring peas have finished producing, eggplant is a worthy summer successor.

Another option for succession planting is to plant from seed. Sowing new seeds every few weeks ensures a continuous crop. Don't forget you can always start seeds indoors. By staggering planting times, you'll continually have a new crop of edibles ready to be planted every few weeks. This works best for plants with a short and fast growing season. In addition to the crops already listed, consider onions, lettuces, or radishes.

In fall, kale is a welcome addition to the vegetable garden.

Follow the Swap-Out Strategy

Towering burgundy amaranth sets off both edibles and neighboring ornamentals.

If you currently have an established planting bed, you may not know how or where to begin incorporating edibles. The technique of creating top, middle, and bottom layers used in narrow ornamental beds works with edibles as well. An easy way to start is to consider adopting a one-for-one swap-out strategy.

For example, if your goal is to plant a tree, why not choose a fruit tree? If a midsized deciduous shrub is next on your list, perhaps a blueberry or currant would be a perfect choice. If annual flowers are what you prefer, instead of zinnias, select violas or nasturtiums to add color and taste to your salads. The main thing to remember is to plant edibles near ornamentals that have similar light and water requirements.

If you want to swap out a substantial plant in your garden bed, one that currently provides height and structure, consider using taller varieties of edibles. Examples include artichokes, cardoons, tomatoes, 'Golden Bantam' sweet corn, or 'Tuscan Blue' rosemary. More exotic choices include amaranth; although their leaves can be harvested for salads, their attractive foliage and flowers are enough of a reason to include them in your garden. Currants also provide beauty as well as food; choose 'Ben Lomand' for its black berries or 'Red Jade' if you prefer red berries. Just remember, when you're mixing edibles with other ornamentals, make sure they receive enough sunlight.

Blueberries on the Bottom

Dwarf varieties of blueberries are a terrific choice for the bottom layer of a narrow border. With white blossoms in spring and red foliage in fall after berries are harvested, 'Top Hat' delivers multiseason interest. Blueberries need acidic soil and good drainage to thrive, so consider planting them in small containers when garden conditions are less than ideal.

When swapping out midsized plants in the middle layer of a planting bed, we love plants that add a shot of color contrast with their fruit or foliage. Favorites include eggplant, with its beautiful dark purple flowers and foliage, and 'Numex Twilight' hot peppers, whose brilliant hues of red, yellow, and orange can bring a garden bed to life. And nothing beats the bright, multicolored stems of 'Rainbow' Swiss chard.

Another swap we like is replacing some of the smaller annuals in the bottom layer of a bed with vegetables or herbs. Low-growing edibles are easily tucked into nooks and crannies around perennials and evergreens. Good choices include herbs that can be harvested a few sprigs at a time such as parsley, chives, and thyme. For foliage color, try purple-hued radicchio or 'Opal' basil with its beautiful burgundy foliage. The white flowers or juicy red fruit of low-growing strawberries is unsurpassed—unless it's by a riotous mix of hot-colored nasturtiums.

Choose low-growing blueberries for the front of an ornamental border.

Edibles That Double as Ornamentals

As designers, we rely on a wide range of foliage and flowers to give each garden color, shape, and form. Edibles are no exception, and when thoughtfully chosen they can play the same important role in your garden. Edible flowers come in a wide range of colors, making them easy to include in just about any garden.

If you want to cool your garden down a bit, you can't go wrong with the blue, star-shaped flowers of a borage plant. On the opposite side of the color spectrum, the bright orange petals of calendula flowers wake up a garden during colder months and are a popular ingredient in teas and other herbal remedies. Multicolored violas come in a range of colors, from white to purple and just about everything in between. They are one of the easiest annuals to grow and add a colorful note both to your garden and your salad bowl.

Besides adding beauty to the garden and food to the table, growing your own edibles means you control how they are cultivated. Growing your own vegetables not only lowers your food bill, but knowing your food is pesticide-free and safe brings you peace of mind.

When filled with cream cheese, nasturtiums make a tasty treat for kids.

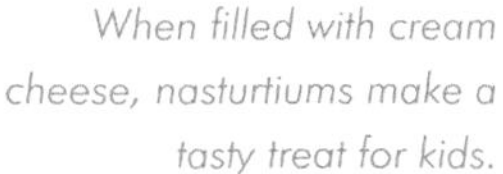

One of our favorite mantras is that plants in small spaces need to perform double duty. When designing a garden, we search out plants that serve more than one purpose, whether they're edible or ornamental. For that reason, we're drawn to edibles that combine a bountiful harvest with characteristics that make them stand out from the crowd.

An alternative to more traditional vegetables, capers thrive in containers.

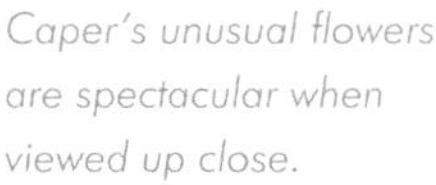

An herb garden is one of the easiest places to go beyond the ordinary. There's an abundance of interesting varieties of herbs that provide unusual foliage without sacrificing favor. Foliage we can't get enough of includes the chartreuse leaves of 'Lime Thyme', the white and green leaves of variegated oregano, and the purple, white, and green leaves of 'Tricolor' sage.

Caper's unusual flowers are spectacular when viewed up close.

Although, for the most part, we've focused on vegetables, fruit, and herbs that are widely grown, seeking out edibles with a more unusual pedigree can elevate your garden above the ordinary. For example, if your only experience with capers is fishing them out of a briny jar, consider adding a caper bush to your garden. Capers thrive in pots, making them an excellent choice for small-space gardens. Not only is this plant attractive enough to grow as an ornamental, but growing your own is also one of the few ways to enjoy this gourmet treat fresh from the garden.

Fruit Trees for Gardens of Every Size

Dwarf Columnar Trees

Is anything better than a tart apple or juicy orange plucked right from your own tree? Small-space gardens typically don't have the room for full-sized fruit trees, but that doesn't mean your only source for fresh fruit is the grocery store or farmers' markets.

There is a large range of dwarf or columnar fruit trees available. As garden sizes shrink, growers continue to graft high-performing fruit trees varieties onto dwarf rootstock. Just about any full-sized fruit tree is also available in a smaller size. Compact fruit trees to consider include 'Black Jack' fig, 'Compact Stella' cherry, 'Pix-Zee' peach, 'Paradise' pear, and dwarf 'Meyer' lemon trees, but do your research to determine the best options for where you live. Your local Master Gardener office or University Extension Service can provide a list of what grows well in your area.

Some varieties have even been bred to maintain a narrow form—in fact, there are several fruit trees that only grow a few feet wide. Trees like this are the perfect choice for shallow garden beds or narrow courtyards and balconies that lack space even for a dwarf cultivar. Besides providing a harvest of tasty fruit, tall trees like this add a vertical dimension to a garden. 'Scarlet Sentinel', 'Golden Sentinel', and 'North Pole' apple trees and the 'Weeping Santa Rosa' dwarf plum tree are among the most popular cultivars.

A columnar apple tree fits into the tightest of spaces.

Standards

Standards, affectionately known as "lollipop trees," are another excellent way to incorporate height into both small planting beds and containers. The term "standard" refers to any plant grafted to an erect stem so that it grows into a treelike form. Many varieties of citrus, olive, pineapple guava (*Feijoa*), and pomegranate trees are grown as evergreen standards. In addition to offering a summer harvest of fruit, they provide year-round interest—a boon to small-space gardeners.

When growing edible standards, keep in mind that they'll require more maintenance than ornamentals. They need more frequent and exacting pruning to retain their shape and to produce more fruit, as well as more frequent feeding.

Almost anything can be grown as a standard—even grapes.

Standard Care

Standard trees must be repotted with fresh soil every few years to completely replenish the soil's nutrients and to maintain the health of the tree. Prune the tree and roots every one to two years during its dormant period to maintain the size of the tree and prevent the roots from becoming rootbound.

Symmetrical espaliered Asian pears have a formal look.

Espalier

Roughly translated, the French word *espalier* means "shoulder support," and the term refers to the practice of training any plant with long and flexible branches to grow flat against a wall. This is done via hooks and wires, and plants are usually—although not always—trained in a geometric pattern. Certain fruit trees such as apples, cherries, and pears actually produce more fruit when espaliered, as the horizontal growth spurs the plant to produce more buds than it normally would.

Espaliers are ideal for narrow beds, courtyards, or anywhere a sunny wall exists; training your fruit trees in this manner is an excellent, space-saving technique for incorporating more edibles into a garden. Even a small-sized espalier provides delightful vertical interest. While espaliered fruit trees have traditionally been trained into formal patterns, they are equally at home in more casual gardens.

Why settle for a wall when you can create an entire house out of pears?

The association of espaliered fruit trees with formal gardens is understandable. The careful geometry of a pear or apple tree trained in this way makes it right at home amidst the symmetrical plantings common in traditional landscapes.

But we've found espaliered fruit trees to be more flexible than that. An espalier tree will tend to take on the characteristics of the garden that it is planted in. When surrounded by ornamentals or vegetables with a looser, carefree habit, they'll reflect that casual style and seem right at home.

If you have the space, there's no need to limit yourself to just walls. Once you develop the technique for growing edibles against a flat surface, you can experiment with more creative ideas. Fruit trees can be trained in an espalier pattern on just about any kind of frame. If there's a flat surface with enough sunlight, there's no reason you can't experiment with edibles there!

This espalier is right at home in a casual kitchen garden.

Reuse and Recycle

Creative Containers

A strawberry ready for harvest.

Not only are edible gardeners growing vegetables in new ways, but they're also reinterpreting what a container can be. If you're a DIYer, a trip to the hardware store may be all that is necessary to create your own interpretation of a vertical edible garden. Ordinary PVC pipe, whether purchased or left over from an irrigation project, makes an excellent vertical wall container. Drill drainage holes in the pipe, attach it to a fence or wall, fill it with a mixture of potting soil and chicken manure, and hook it up to an irrigation system.

Strawberries are ideal for this type of system as their shallow root systems thrive in tight quarters, not to mention that they look charming trailing down the sides of their narrow home. Other edibles such as herbs or lettuce will work as well. Just ensure that the roots are not too big and that the form of the plant won't be too constricted.

Reclaimed PVC pipes are used to build a strawberry tower.

Small spaces force gardeners to reinterpret how edibles are grown, which can result in some creative approaches. If your goal is to tread more lightly upon the planet, household items can be repurposed to form the structure of a vertical garden.

Just about any product can be used, provided there's adequate drainage. However, not all materials are appropriate for growing food. Avoid anything that might be coated with lead-based paint or other corrosives, as the roots from your edibles may absorb these chemicals and contaminate your produce.

An industrial grade bucket hung on a fence makes an innovative container for growing upside-down tomatoes.

A vintage headboard provides a unique and sturdy trellis for scrambling boysenberries.

Nontraditional Trellises

If you're adding a trellis to support floppy or vining edibles, there are more options available than the traditional wooden trellises available at garden centers. A little color and creativity is all it takes to add a dose of style to your planting beds and containers. An additional benefit of choosing a unique trellis is that it will continue to provide interest throughout the winter months, when most plants are dormant. When you use nontraditional materials in nontraditional ways, you begin to personalize your space, creating a unique garden, one that reflects you.

Simple bamboo stakes are given new life with a bright coat of paint.

An old ladder gains new status when colorful blossoms twine through its rungs.

Do It Yourself

Potato Condo

This potato condo is almost ready for harvest.

Potatoes are the ultimate condo dwellers! A potato's stem will continue to produce as long as it remains covered with soil. By growing up, you're basically manipulating its stem into growing taller and taller, which greatly increases the yield. A simple 4- x 4-foot frame can produce up to 75 pounds of potatoes when grown in a potato condo. Not only is this an excellent way to control pests and weeds, but it's kid friendly too. After all, what kid doesn't love rummaging through dirt in search of food?

Build the condo frame.

Step 1. Gather Your Tools

- Wood—either new or recycled
- Hammer and nails or screws
- Landscape fabric
- Potting soil and mulch
- Slow-release fertilizer
- Vermiculite or peat moss
- Seed potatoes

Step 2. Build the Box's Frame

You can use either new or recycled wood—just make sure it's neither pressure treated nor painted, as treated wood may contaminate your crop. After building the 4- x 4-foot frame, you have several options for sealing. The bottom can be constructed with wood (don't forget to drill some drainage holes) or left open to the ground. If left open, landscape fabric can be stapled to the bottom board to prevent soil from escaping when deconstructing the condo at harvest time (step 4).

Step 3. Build the Box Even Higher

Using high-quality soil (preferably mixed with compost, a slow-release fertilizer, and vermiculite or peat moss to help with moisture retention), you can now plant your seed potatoes under a layer of soil and wait for them to sprout. After a few weeks they'll begin to grow. Allow the stems to reach 4 inches. Cover 3 inches of the exposed stem with soil, leaving 1 inch exposed. At this point, nail an additional board onto the box to raise its level, then repeat the process until your potatoes have reached the top layer of their condo.

Potatoes grow incredibly fast. Pay close attention and don't allow the stems to grow more than 4 inches before covering them with soil. If allowed to grow taller, the stems will stop producing.

Potatoes are a thirsty crop and, depending on the weather, can require daily watering. Ideally, the soil should remain moist, as potatoes become misshapen when allowed to dry out during the growing process. But don't keep them too wet, or they will begin to rot.

As the potatoes grow, add additional siding to hold in the soil.

Step 4. Dismantle the Box and Enjoy

Once they've reached the very top, your potatoes will begin to produce tiny, attractive flowers. When the flowers are done blooming, you can begin harvesting in as little as two weeks. The condo can be dismantled all at once, or you can carefully remove the bottom boards and harvest just a few potatoes at a time.

Ingenious gardeners are creating vertical gardening opportunities everywhere, from containers of edibles grown on tiny balconies to artistically planted arbors that separate one garden room from the next. But the ultimate form of vertical gardening is the living wall.

LIVING WALLS

The revolutionary idea that plants that naturally grow in the ground can be used to craft living walls of greenery has captured our imaginations. Inspired by the amazing multistory versions created by design pioneers like Patrick Blanc, home gardeners are discovering a whole new way to garden—and creating their own versions of living wall art along the way.

(Previous page)
The stunning complexity of a living wall made with succulents.

Despite a lack of soil, some plants can happily survive in the most inhospitable locations.

Living Walls

In the Beginning

Plants thriving without soil, growing up the sides of city buildings, offering shelter for wildlife, providing food—sounds futuristic, doesn't it? Not to Patrick Blanc, the French artist and botanist who is often credited as the father of vertical gardening. Blanc has been creating living walls throughout Europe for decades. This exciting combination of gardening and architecture has only recently made its way to the United States, where it has been enthusiastically received by public parks departments, schools, restaurants, and corporations.

Decades ago, Blanc realized that many plants don't really need soil to grow. In fact, the soil is usually nothing more than a holding place for the plant's roots and necessary nutrients. In environments with year-round water such as the tropics and moderate rain forests, Blanc noticed complex layers of plants growing on surfaces typically thought of as inhospitable, including rocks, cliffs, and tree trunks. This led him to the realization that by using the basic components of hydroponics (a system that provides a constant nutrient-rich water supply), he could create an entirely sustainable living wall on almost any vertical surface.

This living wall brings nature to an otherwise man-made environment.

Environmental Benefits

Living walls increase biodiversity in urban areas, and provide safe refuge for birds, insects, and other wildlife.

In addition to their striking beauty, large-scale urban living walls provide many significant benefits:

- **Space Efficiency:** Areas typically considered "wasted space" can now be turned into gardens.
- **Energy Efficiency:** Both the medium and the plants act as insulation, lowering energy consumption by reducing indoor temperatures in the summer and raising them in the winter.
- **Noise Cancellation:** Living walls act as sound barriers to filter out street noise.
- **Heat Reduction:** Living walls help to reduce the heat island effect that occurs in cities with limited green spaces.
- **Air Quality Improvement:** The structure of the walls allows minute particles of pollution to slowly decompose and become fertilizer for the plants.
- **Water Purification:** When attached to downspouts, the plants and roots filter impurities in storm water runoff.
- **Introduction to Nature:** Those born and raised in urban settings may have little exposure to nature. Living walls can provide that connection.
- **Versatility:** Due to the lack of soil, living walls are lightweight in design, allowing them to be mounted on virtually any vertical surface.

Plant Choices

Air plants (Tilandsia) rely on their leaves to absorb nutrients from the air and rain; their roots are only used to anchor a plant to its host.

A living wall made without soil is one of the most extreme forms of vertical gardening, especially when constructed with nonvining plants. Instead of deep root systems, the plants used have roots that can adapt to grow vertically along the wall.

There are several categories of plants that thrive in these man-made environments. Many sedum and succulent varieties are natural choices, as their small size lends itself to mass plantings. In addition to being compact, they possess very shallow root systems that help them anchor themselves to the living wall's backing.

Living walls can be created indoors as well as out.

All of the plants do not need to be small, however. In fact, a design that includes a range of shapes and sizes will result in a more interesting wall. The loose habit of ferns, orchids, heucheras, and carex grasses, for example, allow them to cascade gracefully down a vertical wall, creating a waterfall effect.

Edibles may also be mixed in with ornamental plants. Assuming they're planted lower down the wall within reach, edibles can be harvested at the appropriate time. If you plan to include them, choose those with soft and pliable stems and shallow root systems.

Basic Components

The basic concept of a living wall is actually quite simple and requires only a few components to build. The frame is the skeleton of the structure and is typically made out of metal or a rot-resistant wood, as either of these will withstand the constant supply of moisture. Besides defining the shape of the wall, the frame must be sturdy enough to support its own weight when planted.

A backboard fastened to the frame acts as a moisture barrier and helps keep the living wall from damaging whatever surface it is attached to. PVC (polyvinyl chloride) or stainless steel is commonly used, as they are both durable and waterproof. Next, a holding sheet made from a thick layer of felt or burlap is attached to the backboard. The plants, seeds, or cuttings are then inserted into this layer.

Irrigation is the most crucial component to the success of the living wall. Using hydroponic methods, a solution of nutrient-rich water is consistently applied to the plants. This provides everything except sunlight that a plant needs to survive.

Soilless Walls for the Home Gardener

Soilless systems were initially created as large-scale art installations in public venues. Their scale is massive; living walls may cover several stories of a building or grow

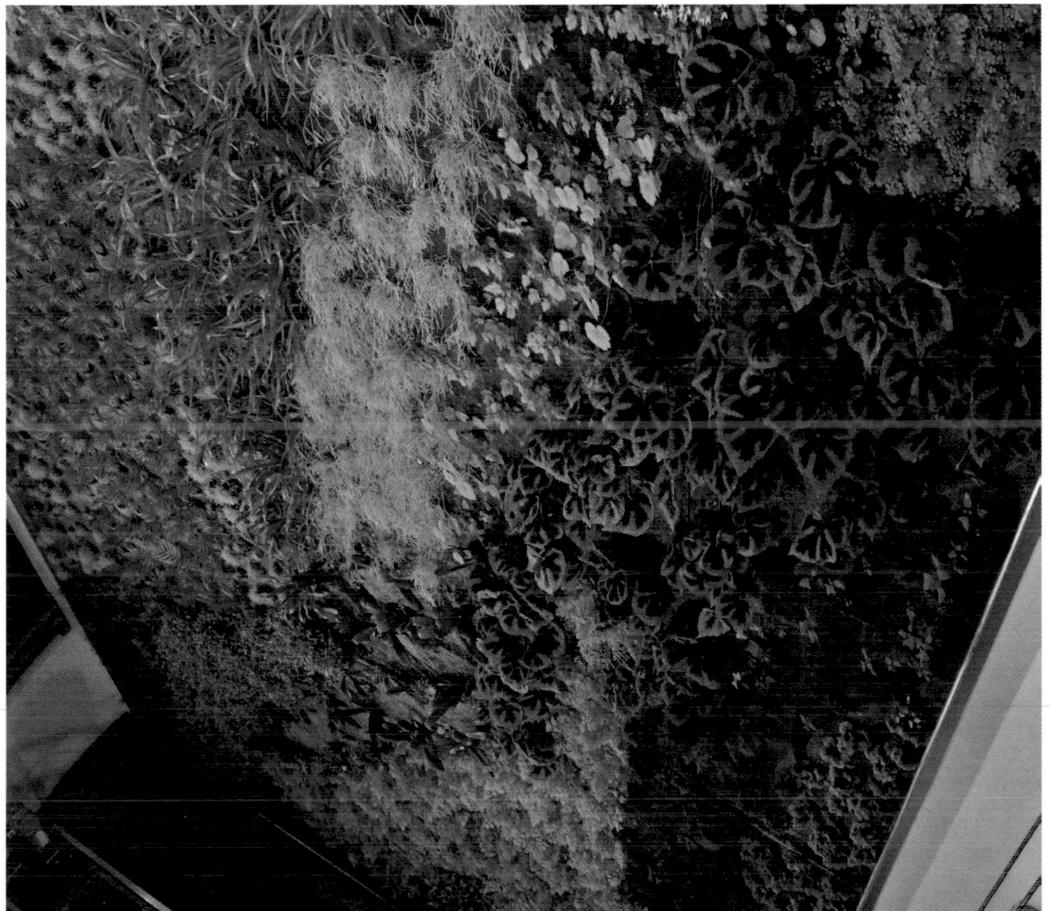

This soilless living wall, created by Patrick Blanc, spans several stories of a parking structure.

up an entire wall in an indoor shopping mall. Home gardeners who embrace these living walls are reinterpreting the system's basic concepts to work within their own gardens.

Because they're essentially a closed system, soilless living walls are often preferred for indoor installations and for oversized public projects. Given their cost and complexity, few home gardeners choose them for modestly sized outdoor projects. If you are considering this type of vertical installation, careful planning and a long-term commitment to upkeep are essential.

Soilless vertical gardens require an extensive irrigation system, as plants must be watered consistently throughout the day. This can quickly add up in terms of cost, time, and effort. There are multiple systems to choose from, so expect to research a range of options in order to determine the best type of irrigation system for your

This soilless wall uses an irrigation system that recirculates water several times a day.

particular project. Fortunately, there are many online sources that provide detailed information on the pros and cons of various systems.

In addition to the meticulous up-front planning and careful construction of your living wall, maintenance is key. Ensuring that the irrigation system is functioning correctly and monitoring the health of the plants requires an ongoing commitment. This is not a project that can be created and walked away from. It should be viewed as a beautiful and ongoing living experiment. Gardeners who prefer a low-maintenance approach should consider other options.

This homemade hydroponic system relies on the nutrient-rich water from the fish tank.

Plant breeder Patrick Fitzgerald created this living wall to gain additional space and privacy.

The smaller scale of this living wall makes it a good choice for residential gardens.

Next-Generation Living Walls

Living Walls for Smaller Gardens

Whether it's due to a lack of space, the desire to create living art, or simply a wish to decorate an unappealing wall, homeowners are looking for new ways to reinterpret Patrick Blanc's grand installations for themselves. One of the simplest ways to create your own piece of living art is to begin with a prefabricated system. While the complexity and cost of soilless systems makes them impractical for many home gardeners, most prefabricated systems use soil as the medium that holds the roots and water, simplifying the entire process.

Systems like these come in many different sizes and formats, including trays, kits, pockets, and panels. Many of them are also modular and can be joined together to form small or large works of art, covering walls of most any size. This flexibility also allows gardeners to experiment with a smaller living wall before committing to a large installation.

Benefits of a Soil-Containing System

Prefabricated soil-containing systems offer many of the same benefits as a soilless system, plus a few extras:

- **Manageable Size:** Even gardeners with very little vertical space can mount one panel to an outside wall. Some of the smallest units are a mere 6 x 12 inches, perfect for the narrowest of walls.
- **Reasonably Priced:** The simplicity of a modular system means it's generally much less expensive to purchase and maintain than a system that relies on hydroponics.
- **Lightweight:** When planted and watered, individual modular units weigh between 15 and 20 pounds, making them suitable for most exterior walls. This manageable weight also makes them easy to move indoors during winter.

Attaching several prefabricated modular units together creates the base for a living wall.

- **Moderate Skill Level:** Prefabricated systems are good for moderately skilled and expert gardeners alike. You can start out small with just one unit and expand as your confidence grows.
- **Green Benefits:** Many of the panel units are constructed with recycled plastics, but more important, they're reusable. They can be planted and replanted over and over again to create different and new gardens.

Reservoir Systems

A reservoir system makes it easier to keep a living wall irrigated, whether watering is done by hand or connected to an irrigation system. The system consists of a prefabricated square or rectangular plastic tray. The tray is made up of a specified number of cells and acts as the frame and support system for the living wall. Individual cells are slanted, which keeps the soil contained and aids in water retention. The angle of each cell allows the water to pool near the back for slower absorption. The slant means each cell has time to absorb the appropriate amount of water before water flows to the next cell, ensuring even distribution and avoiding dry spots.

A reservoir system like this also has the added advantage of being modular. Individual units can be linked together, making it easy to create the exact size wall that you want. Another benefit of these trays is that they can be hooked up to existing irrigation. Some even include their own irrigation, which makes it easier to control the rate at which the living wall is watered.

Most modular units either provide their own irrigation system or are easily connected to an existing system.

Drought-tolerant plants such as succulents require less frequent irrigation.

Hand-Watered Systems

Other types of living wall units are even simpler, consisting of a frame (most commonly made out of rot-resistant wood), a solid backing, and mesh wire to keep the soil in place. Although you might be able to connect irrigation to these frames, they aren't really designed for this and watering will most likely need to be done by hand. To ensure consistent water absorption, it is easier to remove the structure from the wall and lay it on a flat surface to water. Stick with smaller frames, less than 2 feet across, to keep the process manageable. Depending on the plants you choose, deep soaking the unit for thirty minutes every week is the easiest way to maintain your living wall.

Drought-tolerant plants, such as succulents, are an ideal choice for a simple structure like this. Not only can they go for longer periods without water, but their shallow root systems mean they can tolerate the meager amount of soil contained in a smaller frame. Because of their small size, we classify these simple hand-watered systems as living wall art rather than as living walls. Inexpensive and relatively easy to care for, this system is an excellent choice for the home gardener looking for an easy way to add a unique vertical element to the garden. To make the process even simpler, some systems even include the succulents and can be purchased online.

Before and after: Overlapping pocket systems allow maximum flexibility for covering large walls or fences.

Pocket Systems

Pocket-style systems are generally constructed of a breathable material similar to felt. Because the fabric has the ability to breath, the soil can aerate naturally. This breathability means that less water pools in the pockets while draining, thereby reducing the chances of a plant's death due to root rot.

In a closed container, plants often become root-bound. The breathable fabric in a pocket system allows the roots to sense they've reached the limits of their growing medium, at which point they stop growing. This natural process, known as air pruning, means roots are healthier than in a contained system.

Unlike other systems, whose small compartments limit the type of plants that can be grown successfully, just about any plant will work in a pocket system. Just make sure a plant's size is in proportion to the size of the pocket. The more soil the pocket holds, the bigger the plant it will support.

These pocket systems are equally at home indoors or out.

DESIGN SPOTLIGHT

Designing a Succulent Wall

Although living walls can be constructed from plants ranging from tropical to regionally appropriate natives, succulents have become one of the most popular choices in milder climates. Shallow root systems and low water requirements make them an ideal choice for the demanding conditions of a living wall, while the amazing range of colors, textures, and forms is perfect for creating a showstopping design.

Small Works Too
If construction and maintenance requirements make a large-scale succulent wall impractical, consider a more manageable picture-sized version. Kits are available online or you can make your own.

Hand watering a large-scale wall can be impractical; a drip irrigation system minimizes maintenance.
Planting succulents in waves of color creates a cohesive design and keeps the wall from being overwhelmed by the individual plants.
A mix of shapes and textures provides the contrast that makes this composition a work of art.
Succulents with eye-catching characteristics, like the corkscrew shape of Crassula corymbulosa offer interesting detail when the wall is viewed more closely.

In warmer climates, tropical plants thrive year-round in this soilless living wall.

Planting a Living Wall

Plant Choices

Succulents are available in a wide range of colors, sizes, and textures.

With its geometric form and soft green leaves tinged with pink, this succulent is a dramatic addition to a living wall.

In warmer and indoor climates, there are many categories of plants that thrive in soil and soilless vertical wall systems. For a tropical effect, nothing beats the look of a vertical wall filled with bromeliads, orchids, and air plants. For larger plants like these, don't forget to match the size of the cell or pocket with the size of the plant's root system.

If your wall will be in the shade, consider planting it with smaller varieties of ferns and heucheras. For sunny walls, we recommend a mix of ornamental grasses. Their colored foliage and fine textures bring a dramatic cascading effect to your living wall. Responsive to the slightest breeze, grasses add another desirable element to your living wall: movement. Carex grasses are a perfect choice as they're available in many colors and in milder climates are considered evergreen. Other small and tidy grasses with vibrant colors include fescues such as *Festuca glauca* 'Elijah Blue', which has steely blue foliage, and the jet black foilage of mondo grass (*Ophiopogon planiscapus* 'Nigrescens').

Succulents are a natural choice for living walls due to their tight, compact forms, shallow root systems, and low water requirements. In addition, succulents have a unique way of propagating that adds a special dimension to a living wall. Within a few months, the main plant will begin to produce small babies on long, thin stems, called "pups." These pups can be left to either reroot onto the wall or be cut off. Once removed, set them aside to let their ends dry and seal over for a few days. This process is known as "hardening off." Once their ends have sealed, they can either be replanted in your wall unit or elsewhere in your garden. This constant production of offspring enhances the "living" aspect of your wall, as the wall slowly changes in shape and form.

In milder climates with little frost, succulents in the *Crassula*, *Echeveria*, and *Senecio* genuses will provide you with endless choices in color, size, and shape. In climates with colder winters, hardier *Sedum* and *Sempervivum* are the best choices for surviving freezing temperatures. All will thrive with filtered sunlight. They are excellent to form the foundation of your design, whether you want a composition that's energizing or calming, geometric or completely random.

Plant Design for Living Walls

Living walls are like a piece of living art. A well-designed wall is a cohesive composition from a distance, while closer inspection reveals a wealth of intricate detail.

Cool colors keep this wall green and serene.

Some of the same principles used in traditional planting design are applicable to a living wall. One that we find particularly appropriate is the concept of contrast. Use this underlying principle as a guideline when choosing plants for texture, color, and form.

Arranging plants to highlight the contrast between different textures will result in a dynamic composition. This is particularly true if you've chosen a monochromatic color palette. For walls that rely on larger-scale plants such as grasses or ferns, the contrast in texture will be apparent from a distance. Grouping plants with similar textures together will help the wall read from farther away. Conversely, if your wall is built from small plants, such as succulents, texture will be more apparent up close. For maximum effect, place smooth succulents next to those that are spikey or mounding. If you are designing with succulents in a tray system, you will find it easier to lay out your design on a flat surface, but the plants may require several months to establish themselves before they can be attached to a wall.

Foliage and flower color is another opportunity to create contrast. In large gardens, plants are often planted in drifts or swaths. This creates a mass that allows the garden to make an impression from a distance. It's an effective technique, because too many colorful plants packed into the same space can result in a garden with a chaotic appearance. Apply the same principle to your wall by planting in waves of color. The amount of contrast you create will depend on the effect you are trying to achieve. If your goal is restful and serene, then stick with shades of green, white, and silver. Brighter colors with higher contrast, such as oranges, reds, and yellows, will bring more energy to your wall.

A mix of form, color, and texture create a dynamic living wall.

The geometric shape of this living wall is a result of combining succulents with similar shapes, sizes, and colors.

Contrasting a plant's form applies primarily to walls created with succulents or other tight, compact plants. Succulents are a popular choice for a living wall for good reason. In addition to being naturally well adapted to the stresses of vertical gardening, they come in a range of textures, colors, and forms. Contrasting small, tight clusters of plants in the *Sempervivum* genus with the geometric shapes of those in *Crassula* adds yet another layer of interest to the composition.

Caring for a Living Wall

How Long Will a Living Wall Last?

A living wall has more in common with a piece of living art than it does with a traditional garden. And as such, it won't last forever. The unique growing conditions of this type of garden will shorten a plant's natural lifespan. Recognize up front that periodically replacing plants will be a regular part of maintenance.

Plants that grow vertically have to cope with specific stress points not experienced by their counterparts that grow in the ground. For example, a wall module's small cells mean less soil and less room for roots, resulting in stunted plant growth. Less soil also means the cell will dry out more quickly. Consequently, nutrients are used up at a higher rate than they would be in a traditional container.

Another challenge of growing vertically is inconsistent lighting. Plants at the top tend to receive more sun than those at the bottom, and larger plants may cast shade

Expect to periodically replace plants.

over those lower down on the wall. If the plants you've chosen allow it, periodically rotating the wall will reduce the problems uneven lighting can create.

It's also important to pay attention to the soil in your living wall. After a few years, the soil becomes compacted and you'll notice a condition called "soil slump." This is when the soil is doing exactly that—slumping down toward the bottom of the cell or frame.

Finally, maintaining a consistent supply of water is crucial. Check hardware regularly, as occasionally pumps break down and emitters get clogged. If left unchecked, within a few days of any malfunction, plants begin to die.

Will It Last?

Don't forget the "living" aspect of your living wall—nothing lasts forever! Typical low-tech wall units have a lifespan of three to five years. However, as most wall units can be reused, you'll be able to plant them over and over again.

Maintenance

As you've most likely realized by now, living walls require more frequent maintenance than typical containers. You can help your wall live a long and healthy life by remembering to (1) regularly check for clogged irrigation emitters; (2) apply weekly applications of fertilizer, diluted to one-fourth to one-half strength; and (3) rotate the wall a few times throughout the year for consistent lighting and growth.

You may also need to dismantle the wall after several years and start over again with fresh soil. This can be a time-consuming process, but a fun one as well. Taking apart your living wall gives you the chance to start over, keeping the plants that thrived as well as trying new ones.

The placement of your living wall is important. Because of the stressful growing environment, even the hardiest varieties of plants will need to be located in a somewhat protected location. Plants that usually thrive in full sun will perform better with less, and should be planted in partial sun. In fact, no matter what plant you choose, full sun (six hours a day or more) is not advised. Consider placing your living wall on an east-facing wall, where it will be protected from the late afternoon's harsher light and receive no more than four to six hours of direct sun a day.

Maintenance plays a critical role in a successfull living wall. With its spent succulents left to linger on after their time has passed, this imaginative sculpture has lost some of its luster.

The perennials in this modular unit survive snowy winters with minimal die-off, thanks to the protection provided by the roof's overhang.

Overwintering

What happens to your living wall when winter arrives? If you live in a milder climate and appropriate plants are chosen, your wall might be just fine living outside year-round. It's important to remember that in cold temperatures a plant's root system needs to stay hydrated; otherwise it can quickly dry out and die. It may seem counterintuitive, but it is important to keep those plants watered. Hanging your living wall under an overhang will help protect it from frosty temperatures, but in extremely cold temperatures it should be brought inside. It can either be brought indoors and placed in a bright and sunny location, or placed in a greenhouse. Luckily, most units are fairly lightweight and easy to remove, making overwintering a snap.

For walls that are too large to move, plant with hardy perennials that can withstand normal winter temperatures, realizing that you may need to replace a few each spring. Although they are often designed with exotic species, as the concept of living walls becomes more mainstream, using native and other regionally appropriate plants will become increasingly common. This allows oudoor walls to thrive in a greater range of climates. You'll also need to remember to occasionally water these walls (especially if a cold snap is expected), as they will dry out quickly, resulting in the plants' death.

A completed Gladiator Garden overflowing with eggplant, thyme, scallions, and peppers.

Do It Yourself

Gladiator Garden

Vertical gardens don't need to be complicated. DIY gardener Jim Martin found the inspiration and most of the materials for this homegrown wall planter on a trip to his local home-improvement store. Not only do we love the colorful vertical garden he created, but we also love that he named his creation after the brand of tracking hardware he used for the project. Who says vegetable gardening isn't manly?

Use a tracking system to attach the baskets to the fence.

Step 1. Gather Your Tools

- Wire-mesh hanging basket with a tracking system (the basket and tracking system may be sold separately)
- Mounting hardware appropriate for the type of wall or fence you'll be using
- Coconut fiber or felt
- Spray paint
- Potting soil and mulch
- Vegetables, herbs, or annuals with a shallow root system

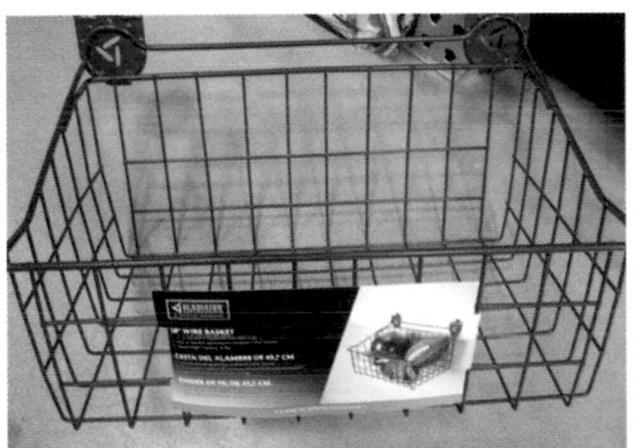

Mesh baskets are readily available from home-improvement stores.

Step 2. Prepare the Baskets

Spray paint the basket, tracking hardware, and coconut fiber or felt. Once everything has dried, line each basket with coconut fiber and attach the track to the fence or wall. When installing two levels of baskets, place them far enough apart to prevent a top planter from shading a lower one.

Cobalt blue color makes the completed baskets a standout.

Step 3. Plant and Maintain

Shallow containers dry out quickly in full summer sun. Unless they will be watered daily, consider placing your baskets in part sun. Choose shallow rooted vegetables such lettuces, radishes, herbs, or annuals to fill your garden. Once you've planted the containers, cover with a layer of mulch to help retain the moisture. Smaller containers also require regular applications of fertilizer, particularly if you are planting heavy feeders like vegetables and annuals. When the growing season is over, the tracking system makes it easy to remove the baskets and prep them for next year's garden.

As you've discovered by now, vertical gardens come in many different forms: from traditional arbors, to gardens planted in gutters, to living walls. One style of vertical gardening can look very different from another. For that reason, instead of grouping plants together by type, we've organized our plant picks by design solution. From climbing roses to decorate a cottage garden

PLANT PICKS

arbor to the best succulents to fill your living wall, we've shared some of our favorite plant choices for a range of garden needs. We've even highlighted a superstar plant from each category that we feel does an outstanding of meeting our standards of disease resistance, reliability, multiseason interest, or superb blooming power. Container gardeners should be sure to check out the last four pages where we share some container garden planting plans.

Vines for Balconies and Courtyards

We'll let you in on a little secret: many vines quickly turn into thugs. While that might not be a problem in large gardens, in small spaces this can rapidly result in a chaotic, overgrown space. In smaller gardens where plants are viewed up close, everything about them needs to shine: we demand fabulous foliage, spectacular blooms, and subtly delightful fragrance. To earn a spot on our favorites list, we expect these vines to be on their best behavior at all times. Not only must they be disease resistant—no blackspot or mildew allowed—but thorns and messy berries are strictly forbidden. And definitely no unruly tendrils reaching out to grab at unsuspecting gardeners!

1. Superstar Performer: *Clematis* 'Arctic Queen'

USDA Zones 4–9

Sun to Part Sun / Moderate Water

We love all clematis, but what makes this one of our favorites is its 8- to 10-foot compact size. Beginning in spring, it's covered with dramatic 5-inch white double flowers that look crisp and clean against its dark green, mildew-resistant foliage. In winter, pruning is a snap, as this variety blooms on both new and old wood.

2. *Passiflora sanguinolenta* 'Maria Rosa' (Passion Vine)

USDA Zones 8–11

Sun to Part Sun / Moderate Water

This 8-foot evergreen vine has slender stems with interesting 2- to 3-inch leaves that are shaped like bat wings. From spring through fall, it's covered with delicate coral pink flowers. It's especially nice in close quarters where both the blooms and the leaves can be truly appreciated.

3. *Thunbergia alata* 'Sunny Lemon Star' (Black-eyed Susan Vine)

Annual in most USDA Zones

Full Sun / Moderate Water

Cheery yellow blooms are the highlight of this fast-growing annual vine that tops out at 10 feet. Count on it to cover your trellis with loads of 1-inch flowers from early summer to the first frost. This particular shade of yellow complements many other colors in the garden.

4. ***Lablab purpureus*** **(Hyacinth Bean Vine)**

USDA Zones 9–11
or grow as an annual
Full Sun / Moderate Water

A very fast climber to 12 feet, this vine bears clusters of purple-pink flowers that age to muted shades of lilac and white. As the blooms mature, they turn into glossy, dark burgundy bean pods. Note that some references list these beans as edible, while others list them as mildly toxic.

5. ***Lonicera xylosteoides*** **'Clavey's Dwarf' (Dwarf Honeysuckle)**

USDA Zones 4–9
Sun to Part Sun / Low Water

Love honeysuckle, but don't have the space? This compact variety grows to just 6 feet and blooms from late spring through summer with the same showy, pink and white, lightly fragrant flowers as its larger cousin. Once established, it's tolerant of drought, heat, and humidity.

Eye-Candy Blooms

Vines add so much personality to a garden. The careful gardener contemplates size, form, habit, and a host of other considerations before making a choice. But sometimes, what's really needed is a jolt of color and a truly unique bloom to wake a garden up! These vines are guaranteed to stop people in their tracks. Each sports massive amounts of blooms, unusual flowers, or a combination of both. If treated as annuals, most are appropriate for a broader range of zones.

1. Superstar Performer: *Aristolochia durior* (Dutchman's Pipe)

USDA Zones 4–10

Part Sun to Shade / Moderate Water

Native to the eastern United States, this fast-growing 20- to 30-foot evergreen vine has beautiful 4- to 10-inch heart-shaped leaves followed in spring by unusual 1½-inch purple and yellow flowers that are shaped like a smoking pipe. Best appreciated up-close, this plant is a favorite among children and adults alike.

2. *Cobaea scandens* (Cup and Saucer Vine)

USDA Zones 9–11

Full Sun / Moderate to High Water

This fast-growing, tender perennial vine quickly grows to 20 feet. Summer through fall, it's covered with dramatic, rose-colored, cup-shaped flowers. As an added bonus, it's resistant to most pests.

3. *Gloriosa superba* (Gloriosa Lily)

USDA Zones 8–11

Sun to Part Shade / Moderate Water

Reaching a mere 4 to 6 feet in height, gloriosa lily is the perfect size for small gardens. But small doesn't mean demure. Dramatic flowers in sunny shades of yellow, orange, and red bloom for up to eight weeks in summer. Gloriosa lilies are planted as bulbs, which make them easily available from online nurseries. Gardeners in colder climates can still enjoy this unique garden specimen—simply dig up the bulbs and overwinter them in moist peat moss.

4. *Kennedia nigricans* (Black Coral Pea)

USDA Zones 8–11

Sun to Part Sun / Low Water

Elegant black and yellow blooms cover this small perennial vine from spring through summer. Growing quickly to an ultimate size of 3 feet tall by 1 to 5 feet wide, its compact form makes it ideal for smaller garden containers. One of the few plants that sports true black flowers, this vine is perfect for up-close viewing.

5. *Millettia reticulata* (Evergreen Wisteria)

USDA Zones 9–11

Sun to Part Sun / Low Water

Unlike its thuggish cousin Chinese wisteria, this evergreen variety tops out at only 20 feet, making it a good choice for most gardens. From summer into fall, this well-behaved vine drips with purple-red flowers with an unusual, camphor-like fragrance.

Climbing Roses

To make it into our top-five list, a climbing rose has to meet some tough criteria. First and foremost, it must be disease resistant. Who wants to worry about blackspot, mildew, or rust on their roses when there are so many hardy varieties available today? Repeat bloom, knockout color, or fantastic fragrance round out our list of requirements.

1. Superstar Performer: 'Sally Holmes'

USDA Zones 5–9
Full Sun / Moderate Water

There's a reason this old-fashioned beauty is still planted in so many gardens. Who can resist its abundant display of pale apricot buds that open to creamy, single-petal flowers? Reaching 10 to 15 feet, this rose blooms heavily throughout spring and summer. Rose hips follow in winter, making for a year-round charmer.
As an added bonus, 'Sally Holmes' has a very long vase life.

2. 'Dreamweaver'

USDA Zones 6–9

Full Sun / Moderate Water

This medium-sized climber reaches a maximum height of 12 to 14 feet. It blooms prolifically, with clusters of pale pink flowers growing on the ends of canes that arch gracefully downwards with the weight of the flowers. This rose's spicy apple fragrance adds a subtle perfume to the garden.

3. 'Jacob's Robe'

USDA Zones 6–9

Full Sun / Moderate Water

This rose is the hardier cousin of well-known 'Joseph's Coat'. Like its popular relative, it sports large semidouble flowers that vary in color from light yellow to apricot to pink. Quickly growing to 10 to12 feet, it has a delightful spicy fragrance and a long bloom time.

4. 'Climbing Eden'

USDA Zones 6–9

Full Sun / Moderate Water

Reaching 10 to 14 feet, this rose's blooms are both spectacularly oversized and neatly formed. Their charming habit is to nod downward, as if begging to be admired from below.

5. 'John Cabot'

USDA Zones 3-9

Full Sun / Moderate Water

Part of the Canadian Explorer series that includes plants bred to withstand harsh Canadian winters, this hardy climber grows a modest 6 to 8 feet and has lightly fragrant, deep red, double flowers. It puts on a spectacular show in June and then blooms sporadically throughout summer.

Exclamation Points

Vertical evergreen plants (also known as fastigiates) are an excellent way to add a focal point to your garden. We think of them as exclamation points, as their purpose is to punctuate the landscape with a little jolt of excitement. Our favorites are hardy and evergreen with a naturally tidy form that requires minimal pruning and maintenance. Exclamation points serve many functions in a garden: they add depth to the landscape, lead the eye, and provide contrast to traditional shrubs and perennials. But most important, they command attention!

1. Superstar Performer: ***Ilex crenata*** **'Sky Pencil' (Japanese Holly)**

USDA Zones 7–10

Full Sun / Low Water

This very slow-growing Japanese holly reaches a maximum size of 10 feet tall by 3 feet wide and has tall stems covered in small, lustrous, dark green leaves. This very low-maintenance shrub rarely needs pruning and fits into the tightest of spaces.

2. ***Cupressus sempervirens* 'Tiny Tim' (Dwarf Cypress)**

USDA Zones 7–10

Sun to Part Sun / Low Water

This slow-growing cypress reaches 20 feet tall by 3 feet wide over a period of many years. It maintains a much tighter form than other cypresses and holds together well in inclement weather. It's much less likely to splay apart in high winds or light snow, making it a desirable exclamation point in the garden.

3. ***Nandina domestica* 'Royal Princess' (Heavenly Bamboo)**

USDA Zones 6–10

Sun to Part Sun / Low Water

With stiffly upright branches, this fast-growing evergreen shrub reaches 8 feet tall by 3 feet wide in just a few years. Its finely textured leaves are tinged with coppery new growth that turns orange-red in fall. Prolific red berries offer a burst of color in winter.

4. *Juniperus virginiana* 'Prairie Pillar' (Dwarf Juniper)
USDA Zones 4–9
Full Sun / Low Water

Icy blue-green foliage on this tough juniper makes it a stunning vertical accent. It grows to 15 feet tall by only 2 to 3 feet wide and requires only occasional pruning. This juniper makes a very low-maintenance addition to your garden.

5. *Thuja occidentalis* 'Emerald' (American Arborvitae)
USDA Zones 2-7
Sun to Part Sun / Moderate Water

Tolerant of a wide range of soils and humidity, this slow-growing compact evergreen is a perfect choice for smaller gardens. Reaching just 6 to 10 feet tall by 3 to 6 feet wide, it makes a beautiful evergreen accent for small spaces.

Skinny-Space Perennials

If you're looking for vertical plants to bring color and form to narrow garden beds, then you're in the right place. Our favorite performers all have a star quality, whether that's spectacular flower color, architectural grace, or amazing foliage. Not only that, but they're tough and dependable, reliably returning year after year with vigorous growth.

1. Superstar Performer: *Canna indica* (Indian Shot)

USDA Zones 8–11. In colder climates, dig up bulbs and overwinter.

Full Sun / Low Water

The leaves and flowers of the canna come in a dazzling array of colors that add a tropical touch to the garden. This tall perennial quickly grows 3 to 10 feet high by 2 to 3 feet wide. A few of our favorites include 'Pretoria' for its hardiness, 'Black Knight' for its maroon leaves, and 'Panache' for the soft peach color of its blossoms.

2. *Verbena bonariensis* (Purpletop Vervain)
USDA Zones 6–10
Full Sun / Low Water

A magnet for butterflies and hummingbirds, this see-through verbena is 4 feet tall by 2 feet wide. The tall yet airy form of this architectural plant adds vertical interest to a garden bed without adding density. It blooms prolifically from spring through fall in the hottest and driest spots in your garden, but be cautious where you plant it, as it can reseed aggressively.

3. *Calamagrostis acutiflora* 'Karl Foerster' (Feather Reed Grass)
USDA Zones 4–9
Sun to Part Sun / Low Water

This tall and stately ornamental grass didn't win a Perennial Plant of the Year award by accident! Its slender green foliage emerges in spring, ultimately forming a 2- to 3-foot, gracefully arching clump. Late summer through fall, an additional 3 feet of upright golden blooms top the grass. This grass produces sterile seeds, so reseeding shouldn't become a problem.

4. *Anigozanthos* (Kangaroo Paw)

USDA Zones 9–11

Full Sun / Low Water

Kangaroo paw is a knockout choice for mild-climate gardens, combining architectural form with show-stopping flowers. With so many outstanding varieties to choose from, it's hard to pick a favorite, but two that make the top of our list are tall and tough 'Tequila Sunrise' with its brilliant orange-red flowers and 'Harmony' with its cheery yellow blooms. Both varieties bloom nonstop from spring through fall on 4- to 6-foot stalks.

5. *Helianthus salicifolius* (Willow Leaf Sunflower)

USDA Zones 4–9

Full Sun / Low Water

This tall beauty grows 4 to 6 feet tall by 3 feet wide, and is covered with a mass of yellow flowers from late summer through the end of fall. Wispy willow-like leaves surround the tall, slender stems, making the plant a standout vertical accent for the back of the bed.

Edibles with Vertical Impact

Mixing edibles with ornamentals is a trend that's caught on with small-space gardeners who want to have it all. But why not take it a step further and add vertical interest to your garden with edibles attractive enough to double as ornamentals? It's hard to beat vegetables and herbs that taste delicious and offer height, eye-catching color, and dramatic blooms.

1. Superstar Performer: ***Foeniculum vulgare* 'Purpureum'** (Bronze Fennel)

USDA Zones 4–9

Full Sun / Moderate Water

This towering herb grows 6 feet tall by 1 to 2 feet wide. Profuse yellow flowers in fall follow lacey bronze foliage. The anise-flavored leaves are delicious mixed with soups and salads, and if the plant is allowed to go to seed, the leaves can be dried and used throughout the year.

2. *Agastache foeniculum* (Anise Hyssop)

USDA Zones 4–11

Full Sun / Low Water

This edible form of anise hyssop (not to be confused with its ornamental perennial cousins) quickly grows 3 to 5 feet tall by 1 foot wide, and features bright purple flowers throughout summer and fall. Its licorice-flavored leaves can be steeped in warm honey and used as a delicious drizzle over shortcake.

3. *Levisticum officinale* (Lovage)

USDA Zones 5–8

Sun to Part Sun / Moderate Water

This giant in the edible world quickly grows 6 feet tall by 3 feet wide, and has fernlike, dark green leaves and masses of little yellow flowers. This perennial's young leaves taste similar to celery and may be used in salads.

4. *Cynara scolymus* (Artichoke)

USDA Zones 6–11

Full Sun / Moderate Water

Both ornamental and edible, this 4- to 6-foot beauty is at home in any garden. Oversize gray leaves provide both colorful contrast and dramatic architectural value. Its giant purple thistle flowers turn into the edible fruit and are a spectacle to behold. We're particularly fond of 'Violetto'; its slightly elongated artichokes blushed with purple make it a standout in a mixed bed.

5. *Ficus carica* 'Petite Negra' (Fig)

USDA Zones 7–11

Full Sun / Moderate Water

The demure size of this fig tree, which reaches only 3 feet at maturity, makes it the perfect edible solution for your planting bed. Evergreen and resistant to deer, this beautiful tree provides plump and juicy fruit throughout summer.

Tall and Narrow Trees

Many gardeners want a little privacy or seek to block out an unsightly view. When space is an issue, finding a tree that's tall enough to get the job done yet slim enough to fit into a narrow space can be challenging. Our picks not only have the tall and narrow dimensions needed for privacy screening, but are worthy trees in their own right. Whether it's brilliant fall color, an interesting form, or outstanding foliage color, each tree has something special to offer the small-space gardener.

1. Superstar Performer: *Pyrus calleryana* 'Chanticleer' (Ornamental Pear)

USDA Zones 4–9

Full Sun / Moderate Water

Clouds of white flowers in spring, followed by shiny green leaves in summer and blazing foliage in shades of yellow, red, and orange in fall, make this three-season performer one of our favorite screening trees. One of the hardiest in the ornamental pear family, it grows 30 feet tall by approximately 15 feet wide.

2. *Prunus caroliniana* 'Compacta' (Compact Laurel Cherry)

USDA Zones 7–11

Full Sun / Moderate Water

Quickly growing 15 feet tall by 8 feet wide, this evergreen tree or shrub makes an excellent windbreak and provides maximum coverage from neighbors, noise, and wind. We love its unusual scent—its crushed leaves have an aroma like maraschino cherries.

3. *Ginkgo biloba* 'Tremonia' (Maidenhair Tree)

USDA Zones 3–9

Full Sun to Part Sun / Moderate Water

This stunning deciduous tree has distinct, heavily lobed, greenish blue leaves in spring and summer, followed by leaves that turn brilliant yellow-orange in fall. Growing at a slow-to-moderate rate to 50 feet high by 10 feet wide, this tree may grow too large for ultra-small gardens.

4. ***Picea abies*** **'Cupressina' (Norway Spruce)**

USDA Zones 2–7
Full Sun / Moderate to High Water

This evergreen tree grows 15 to 20 feet high but only 3 to 5 feet wide. Bright green needles in spring gradually darken and are followed by 4- to 6-inch light brown cones in fall. Cold-climate gardeners will appreciate this tightly formed tree's ability to holds its shape when covered with snow.

5. ***Azara microphylla*** **(Boxleaf Azara)**

USDA Zones 7–9
Part Sun / Moderate Water

Delicate green and glossy foliage is tightly held on spraylike branches on this narrow yet airy tree. In spring, its small yellow flowers have a mild vanilla scent that lightly perfumes your garden. Reaching 15 feet tall by 4 to 6 feet wide at maturity, it forms a natural espalier with very little training when planted against a wall.

Small Trees for Balconies

When a balcony is your garden, privacy can be hard to come by. Trees with tall, narrow dimensions and roots that can handle being confined to a container are challenging to find. Our picks for this unique garden situation include trees that can handle these less-than-ideal conditions. Not only that, but most can cope with wind and irregular lighting—and still offer the attractive foliage and form that balcony gardeners are looking for.

1. Superstar Performer: *Acer palmatum* 'Shishigashira' (Japanese Maple)

USDA Zones 5–9

Part Sun to Shade / Moderate Water

This unusual specimen of Japanese maple has small yet heavy curled and crinkled leaves that cover short, stubby branches along an upright form. Slowly growing to 10 feet high by 6 feet wide, it withstands significant sun better than most Japanese maples. Its stunning yellow fall color is a bonus.

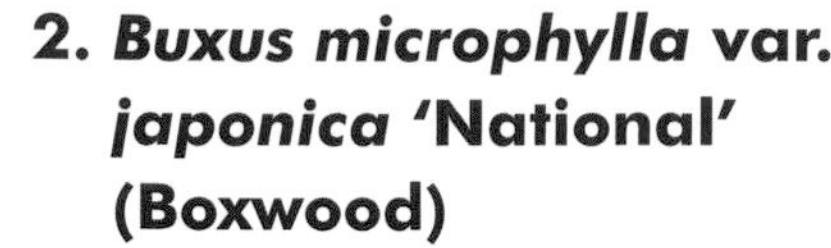

2. ***Buxus microphylla* var. *japonica* 'National' (Boxwood)**

USDA Zones 5–9
Sun to Part Sun / Moderate Water

With its narrow and upright shape, evergreen boxwood makes a dense year-round screen. It reaches 8 feet tall by only 3 feet wide. Its small, glossy, and symmetrical dark green leaves make this a good choice to layer behind more colorful plants. Shallow roots make it a good choice for containers.

3. ***Nandina domestica* 'Umpqua Princess' (Heavenly Bamboo)**

USDA Zones 6–9
Sun to Part Sun / Low Water

Quickly growing to 5 feet tall by 3 feet wide, this upright evergreen shrub turns a beautiful reddish purple color in fall. Bunches of small white flowers in spring and summer, followed by profuse hard, red, berrylike clusters through winter, will keep your balcony garden interesting all year.

4. *Dodonaea viscosa* 'Purpurea' (Purple Hopseed Bush)

USDA Zones 8–11

Sun to Part Sun / Low Water

This evergreen shrub with elongated bronze to maroon leaves grows to 11 feet tall by 5 feet wide, but will be smaller when confined to a container. Spring clusters of pink flowers contrast beautifully with the bronze foliage. The shrub responds well to pruning and makes an excellent windbreak.

5. *Bambusa lako* (Timor Black Bamboo)

USDA Zones 9–11

Sun to Part Sun / Moderate Water

Grown in containers, this bamboo can reach at least 10 feet and provides a dramatic screen or focal point with its thick, upright, clumping black canes. It can tolerate somewhat harsh conditions, as the leaves hold their shape in the wind without shredding.

Succulents for Living Walls

Succulents have taken the gardening world by storm, and for good reason! Available in many colors, shapes, forms, and sizes, these plants are a favorite among gardeners. The varieties listed here are compact in size and form, which make them ideal candidates for living walls. In addition, their shallow root systems allow them to exist comfortably in small amounts of soil. Since living wall units tend to dry out much faster than traditional containers, these hardy and drought-tolerant succulents are the perfect choice.

1. Superstar Performer: *Sempervivum*

USDA Zones 3–11

Part Sun / Low Water

This genus includes the hardiest succulents, many of which can survive snowy winters. Colors include green, brown, yellow, orange, pink, and red—look for plants by color, as named varieties can vary from source to source. Leaves vary as well, from glossy to matte; some have a waxy bloom and some have downy hairs similar to cobwebs.

2. *Echeveria*

USDA Zones 9–11
Part Sun / Low Water

This category is known for its concentric and stemless rosettes that resemble the shapes of flowers. The broad leaves are typically deep blue or gray, or sometimes tipped with red. The leaf margins may be white, giving the rosette a metallic and highly structural quality. Good choices include *E. imbricata, E. elegans,* and *E. secunda*.

3. *Crassula*

USDA Zones 9–11
Part Sun / Low Water

This large genus of succulents contains over two hundred species.
The species range in size from small 1-inch plants to towering 6-foot shrubs. Their stacked, geometric quality adds texture and architectural interest to a living wall. Some of our favorites are *C. corymbulosa, C. expansa,* and *C. rupestris*.

4. ***Sedum*** **(Stonecrop)**

USDA Zones 3–11

Part Sun / Low Water

This is one of the hardiest of the succulent families, with a sedum for just about any USDA zone. Hardy sedums come in an infinite variety of color and form. Colors include green, brown, orange, pink, and red; look for plants by color as named varieties can vary from source to source.

Leaves vary as well, from glossy to matte; some have a waxy bloom and some have downy "hairs" similar to cobwebs. Unlike the mounding shapes typical of other succulents, many sedums possess a trailing habit that brings welcome contrast to a living wall. Their leaves range from a miniscule ¼ inch to 3 inches or more. Some that we like include *Sedum hispanicum*, *Sedum album*, *Sedum* 'Angelina', and *Sedum dasyphyllum* 'Minor' and 'Major'. At left are *Sedum spathulifolium* 'Carnea' and *Sedum spurium* 'Dragon's Blood'.

Themes for Living Walls

Living walls can be designed with just about any small to moderately sized plant. As when designing a traditional garden, working with a theme is a good way to create a cohesive composition. Once you've settled on a style, opt for plants that are able to withstand the stresses inherent in a vertical garden, such as uneven lighting, sparse amounts of soil (if any), and inconsistent moisture levels. Make sure your living wall system contains enough soil to support whatever plants you decide to include. And, of course, your garden has to look good! Choose plants with striking foliage, long-lasting blooms, or interesting texture.

1. Superstar Performer: Native Wall

For a living wall that will thrive, consider using natives. Your wall is more likely to flourish in an already difficult growing environment if you choose plants that actually *want* to grow in your region. By opting for plants that are accustomed to the climate zone, your odds of success are higher and your plant selection at local nurseries is larger. All three systems—pockets, soilless walls, and prefabricated units—are fine for growing this category of plants.

2. Tropical Wall

For a lush, tropical effect, nothing beats the look of a vertical wall filled with bromeliads, orchids, ferns, and air plants. These tropical plants grows best in pocket systems or soilless walls, as their roots require more space than is provided in the small cells of prefabricated units. These plants vary greatly in size, shape, and color. Some of our favorites include hardier choices such as *Pothos, Hoya,* and *Tradescantia*.

3. Edible Wall

If you're planting a living wall that's mainly edibles, remember that those with shallow roots work best, such as lettuces, kales, cabbages, sages, herbs, and trailing strawberries. Leafy lettuces come in so many varieties and colors that you can create a stunning effect by planting a wall entirely in lettuces. All three systems—pockets, soilless walls, and prefabricated units—are fine for growing this category of plants.

4. Perennial Wall

Herbaceous plants, as opposed to those with woody stems, are the best choice for a living wall made from perennials. We suggest mixing foliage plants with flowering perennials. Some of our favorites include heucheras, smaller salvias, helichrysums, begonias, impatiens, and geraniums. All three systems—pockets, soilless walls, and prefabricated units—are fine for growing this category of plants.

5. Grass Wall

Carex and smaller grass varieties are beautiful when massed in a single living wall. Grasses are particularly lovely, as they add movement to the garden, swaying gently in the lightest of breezes. Plants in the hardy *Carex* genus are typically evergreen and are a good choice for year-round color. Foliage we like includes the variegated leaves of *C. oshimensis* 'Everest', the gold leaves of *C. oshimensis* 'Everillo', and the black leaves of *Ophiopogon planiscapus* 'Nigrescens'. All three systems—pockets, soilless walls, and prefabricated units—are fine for growing this category of plants.

Edible Container Combinations

Containers are one of the easiest ways to introduce edibles into a small-space garden. The following combinations rely on dramatic foliage, long blooming flowers, and compact vegetable varieties to maximize yield and impact. By tucking a few blooms or a dramatic ornamental plant in with your produce, you can create a container pretty enough for any garden, even if you never harvest a single leaf or vegetable! Keep in mind that most vegetables require full sun for optimum performance.

A Stylish Combination of Herbs and Ornamentals

Even everyday herbs take on a sophisticated edge when paired with elegant silver foliage and pale pink flowers. Mint is ideal in containers, as its highly invasive roots mean it will take over a traditional herb garden planted directly in the ground. We love the contrast purple varieties of basil add to a container; to help them maintain their color, remove any green offshoots when they appear.

For a contemporary spin, plant in a sleek, metallic container, or opt for a classic look with a European terracotta urn.

Winter Salad Bowl

A salad bowl not only adds color and beauty to a winter garden, but when you plant lettuces that can be harvested a little at a time you'll have salad ingredients that take you from winter into spring. Adding edible flowers makes this container pretty enough to grace a front porch. A lettuce garden like this one thrives in a wide, shallow bowl or a wall hanging system such as Woolly Pockets™.

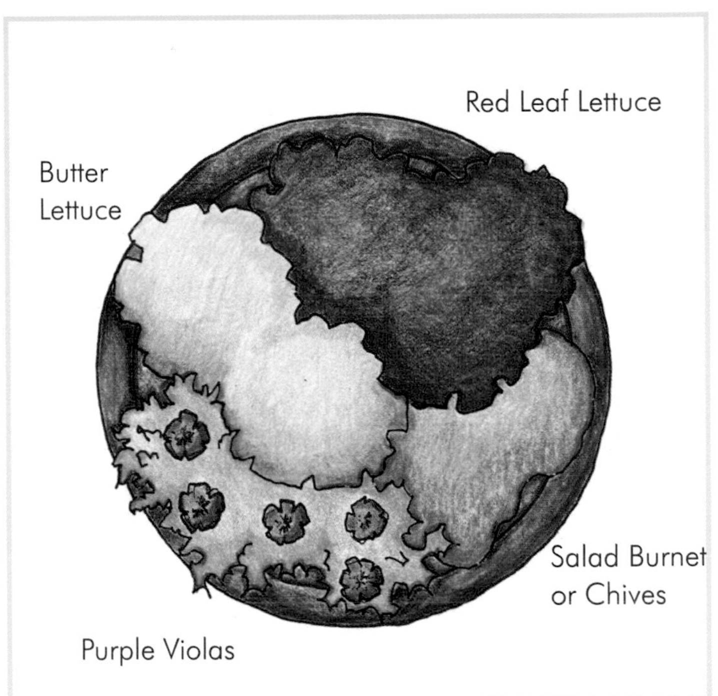

Pizza Garden for a Sunny Patio

Take your pizza to the next level by topping it with fresh Italian herbs and sun-ripened tomatoes from your own garden. We've chosen purple basil for its welcome splash of color, but traditional green basils such as 'Globe' provide more intense flavor. A wide, deep bowl—think pizza-shaped—will ensure the tomato roots have enough space to thrive in this culinary container.

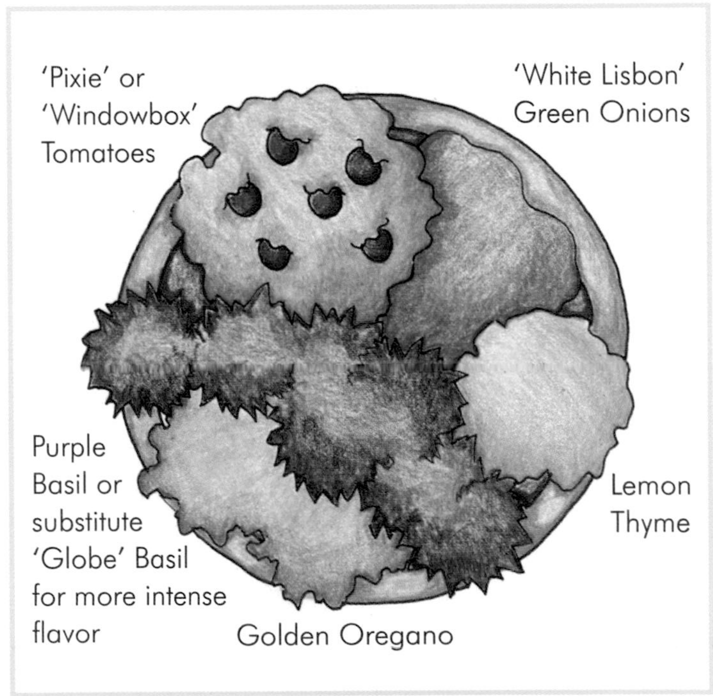

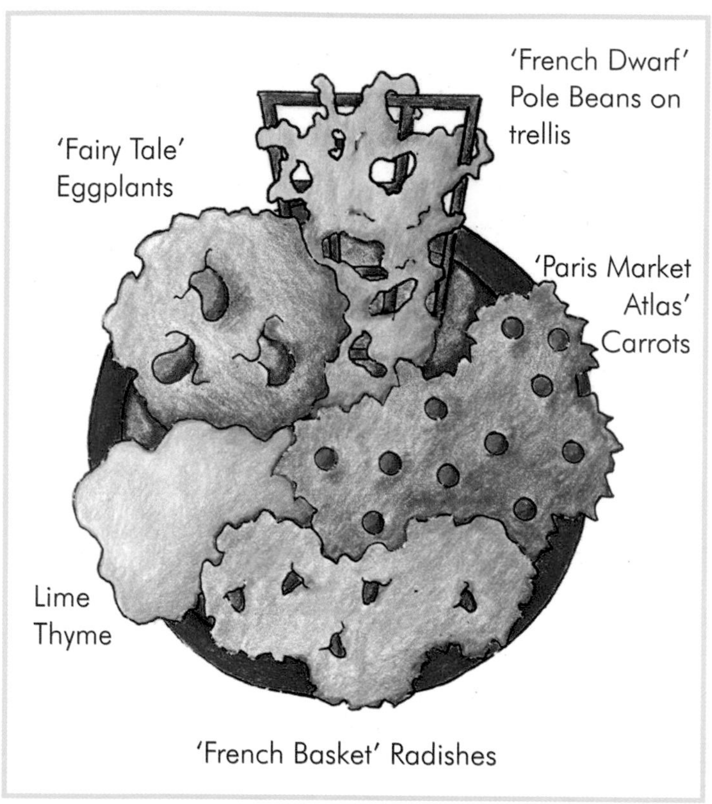

Maximize Your Harvest with Nontraditional Varieties

You'd be amazed at how many vegetables one average-sized container can hold. Utilizing a small trellis and selecting compact varieties allows you to harvest a large selection of edibles in a small amount of space. Starting in spring with early-producing radishes, and going all the way through fall with carrots and eggplants, this hard-working combination provides months of vegetables for your table.

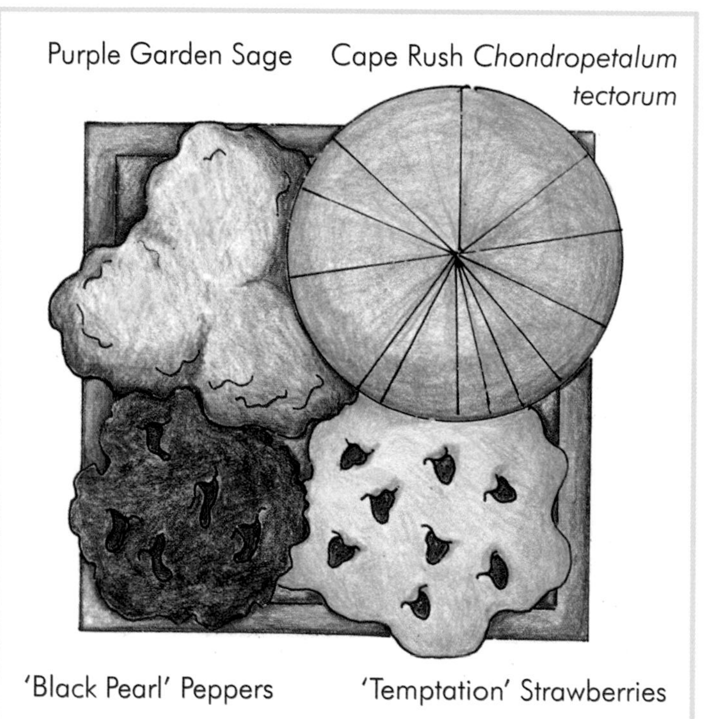

Contemporary Combination Focuses on Foliage

This edible-ornamental combination relies on foliage color and texture for maximum impact. Look for herb and vegetable varieties with unusual leaf color, such as 'Black Pearl' peppers and purple-leafed garden sage, and combine with an architectural ornamental grass like small cape rush. Evergreen grasses and perennial herbs are a good choice to provide a year-round backdrop for annual vegetables. Plant in a geometric-shaped container for a chic and sleek composition.

DISAPPEARING ACT

Minimizing a Roofline

With nothing but an unadorned fence separating her backyard from the house next door, garden designer Laura Schaub realized she needed a solution that would hide her neighbor's prominent roofline, while still leaving plenty of space to create the garden retreat she envisioned. By introducing carefully chosen vertical elements and plants, not only was she able to make the roofline disappear, she created a screening solution so attractive, her new seating area now faces that direction!

Before: *Shallow backyards like this simply don't have the room for large screening trees or traditionally layered planting beds.*

After: *Now, instead of staring at a roofline every day, Laura enjoys her private enclosed garden.*

Besides providing much-needed shade, arbors in small gardens like this one help to frame views, and provide welcome contrast to densely planted beds.

The burgundy leaves of fast-growing purple hopseed bush (Dodonea purpurea) provide year-round color contrast, while colorful purple-red flowers in summer turn this part of the garden into a seasonal focal point.

Shrubs that can be pruned into a small tree shape are a perfect choice to screen unattractive views in a small backyard.

Wisteria trained atop the arbor adds to the garden's cozy charm, and turns a simple patio into an intimate retreat.

AN ISLAND GETAWAY

Tropical Jewel Box

Hoping to capture the exotic feel of an island getaway, the owner of this tiny townhouse courtyard dreamed of a lush garden retreat. Through a mix of different-shaped containers, architectural plants, and thoughtfully chosen vertical elements, a neglected garden was transformed into a colorful reminder of a tropical vacation.

Before: *With only a few plants in containers to brighten up the space, the homeowner had little reason to venture into the garden.*

After: *When space is at a premium, the best solution is often to turn a garden into a room—literally. Tiling the floor creates a base for furniture and a colorful container garden.*

Tall and slender 'Tequilla Sunrise' kangaroo paw makes a vibrant backdrop for a cozy loveseat.

Arranging containers at different heights and choosing a mix of plant textures results in a richly layered garden in a narrow space.

The arbor provides the structure to fill the space from two directions—jewel-toned lamps hang from above, while a narrow fountain and brightly colored coleus fill the floor.

A mix of jasmine for fragrance and clematis for seasonal color create a garden to feed all the senses.

A LEVEL OF SELCUSION

Recovering From a Chainsaw Happy Neighbor

When new neighbors moved in and adopted a "scorched earth" policy of removing every living tree on their property, these homeowners needed a permanent solution to regain their privacy—not to mention hide the newly exposed roofline next door. When a space is too narrow for traditional screening plants to fit, a creative set of vertical solutions is required.

Before: *Because the home's bedrooms are all located on the same side of the house, both privacy and protection from intense summer heat were a priority.*

After: *The new side yard is even better than before, thanks to a clever trellis system.*

A narrow arbor increases privacy by raising the height of the fence while also providing a frame for screening vines to attach to. Adding a structure like this also allows heavier vines or espaliered shrubs to be used than a fence alone could support.

Evergreen, fast growing, and covered with eye-catching red winter berries, pyracantha makes a perfect privacy screen.

While privacy and protection from the sun were the most important goals for this makeover, the homeowner took advantage of the newly planted bed to layer in garden decorations and improve the views from inside.

A tall and narrow decorative pole mimics the narrow form of the plants in this small bed and provides a subtle contrast.

MAKE AN ENTRANCE

An Inviting Entryway

With tight budget constraints, this homeowner's goal was a courtyard makeover with year-round appeal that wouldn't break the bank. By investing in a few vertical focal points and layering plants to make the most of the available space, this entry courtyard was transformed from ordinary to extraordinary.

Before: *With no real focal points, visitors entering the courtyard were most likely to notice the plain walkway, simple gate, and expansive blank walls. Creative layering was needed to redirect the line of sight.*

After: *The once-dull courtyard is now a pleasure to come home to at the end of the day.*

Closed spaces intensify scent. Evergreen and highly fragrant star jasmine vine fills the courtyard with heady fragrance during summer.

By choosing a wall fountain over a freestanding one, the eye is directed "up" while the fountain's slim, vertical shape simultaneously allows layered plantings below.

A 'Meyer' lemon in a "standard" shape not only provides plentiful fruit, but its form allows room for additional plantings beneath, a key to creating a lush garden in a small space.

A decorative trellis provides an elegant, year-round focal point, even when bare of plants during winter.

A GARDEN RETREAT

Post Lawn Makeover

Realizing their existing lawn no longer served a purpose, these empty nesters were ready to transform their backyard into a garden retreat with space for dining, gardening, and other activities. But carving out rooms in such a small garden while simultaneously providing another layer of privacy screening posed a daunting challenge. The solution was the addition of a vertical planting bed in an unexpected place.

Before: *In addition to a lawn that was virtually ignored, the existing oversized screening hedge overwhelmed this small backyard.*

After: *What was once a ho-hum lawn is now a garden filled with garden rooms and overflowing planting beds.*

The dining area is subtly separated from the rest of the garden.

No need for dense hedges! The birch trees function as colorful dining room "walls" and provide another layer of screening from neighboring views.

Even in a narrow bed there's room for personal touches and garden ornaments that provide a splash of contrasting color.

A "moon-shaped" bed filled with vertical plants in the center of the garden separates the outdoor room, enhances privacy, and adds another layer of green to the garden.

Photo & Illustration Credits

All Illustrations are by **Susan Morrison**

PHOTO CREDITS

Linda Anderson: 171 (photo two), 180, 181

Patrick Blanc: 143, 147, 148

Jim Charlier: 130

Shawna Coronado: 54 (photo 1)

Angela Davis: 10, 26 (inset), 33, 74

Sophie deLignerolles: 101

Michelle Derviss: 22 (inset)

Jacki Dougan: 185

Earthbox: 116

Patrick Fitzgerald: 149 (photo two)

Michelle Hamerslough: 111, 125 (photos two and three), 129

Susan Harris: 203

Annie Haven: 86

Diane Chapman Hodges: 178 (photo two)

HolisticForgeWorks: 117

Jayme Jenkins: 122, 123

Gale Jolly: 189 (photo one)

Gardenbeet: 112, 154,160, 199 (photo one)

Fried Kampes: 186 (photo one)

Jeffrey Linn: 133 (inset)

Theresa Loe: 118, 119, 133, 136, 136, 137, 138, 139, 174 (photo one)

Jim Martin: 158, 166, 167, 198 (photo one)

Troy McGreggor: 79

Kerry Michaels: 120, 137 (inset), 197

Susan Morrison: 9, 15, 25 (inset 4), 27, 31 (inset), 76, 83, 85 (inset), 90 (inset), 92, 93, 94, 101, 104 (inset), 125 (photo one), 134, 144, 153, 156 (inset), 159 (photo two), 144, 153, 156 (inset), 159 (photo two), 206

Nori Lamphere: 149 (photo one)

Randy Parker: 172 (photo one)

Kim Parnell: 107

Pam Penick: 39, 46, 99, 183 (photo one)

Jenny Peterson: 89, 95, 96 (inset)

Eva Prokop: 78

Laura Schaub: 71, 88 (inset), 187, 204

Sam Scott: 155

Sarahracha: 177 (photo two)

Peter Seabrook: 97, 114

Dan Sweet: 49 (canna bloom), 145, 182

Rebecca Sweet: 4, 7, 12, 13, 15 (inset), 16, 17, 18, 19, 20, 21, 22, 23, 24, 26, 28, 29, 30, 31, 32, 34, 35, 36, 40, 42, 43, 44, 47, 48, 50, 51, 52, 53, 54, 56 (inset), 57, 58, 59, 62, 63, 64, 65, 66, 67, 68, 69, 70, 72, 73, 75, 80, 81, 82, 84, 85, 87, 90, 91, 96, 98, 99 (inset), 100, 101 (inset), 102, 103, 106, 108, 109, 110, 124, 126, 127, 128, 131, 132, 135, 140, 142, 146, 151, 157, 159, 161, 162, 163, 164, 168, 170, 171 (photo one), 172 (photo two), 173, 175, 176, 178 (photo one), 179, 183 (photo two), 184, 186 (photo two), 188, 189 (photo two), 190 (photo one), 191, 192, 193, 194, 196, 208, 210, 212

VertiGarden: 113, 115, 150, 152, 165

Lieuwe Zander: 199

Resources

Authentic Haven Brand Soil Conditioner Tea: 86, www.ahavenbrand.com

Bright Green Living Wall Planters: 151, www.brightgreenusa.com

Earthbox: 116, www.earthbox.com

Feeney Garden Products: 122, www.feeneygarden.com

Garden Beet: 112, 154, 160, 199 (photo one), www.gardenbeet.com

H. Potter: 84, 100, 103, 211, www.hpotter.com

Succulent Gardens: 91, 141, 144, 153, 156, 159, 161, 194, 195, 196, www.sgplants.com

VertiGarden: 113, 115, 150, 152, 165, www.vertigarden.co.uk

Woolly Pockets: 112, 154, 155, 160, 199, www.woollypocket.com

About the Authors

Meet Rebecca

Rebecca Sweet is the owner of Harmony in the Garden, located in Northern California. Rebecca's signature "Garden Fusion" design style blends her clients' personal desires with regionally appropriate plants. Her gardens have been featured in *Fine Gardening*, *Horticulture*, and *Fine Homebuilding* as well as regional newspapers and publications.

In addition to designing gardens, Rebecca is a featured columnist for *Horticulture*, a contributing author for *Fine Gardening*, and writes design-focused articles for Fiskars®. Rebecca contributes content to online garden sites as well, including Fine Gardening Online, Real Simple Online, and Nest in Style. She is a founding member of the Garden Designer's Roundtable.

It's easy to get to know Rebecca better—chat with her on Facebook or Twitter, or leave a comment on her blog "Gossip in the Garden."

Follow Rebecca on Twitter @SweetRebecca.
Read Rebecca's blog at www.gossipinthegarden.com.
View her design portfolio at www.harmonyinthegarden.com.

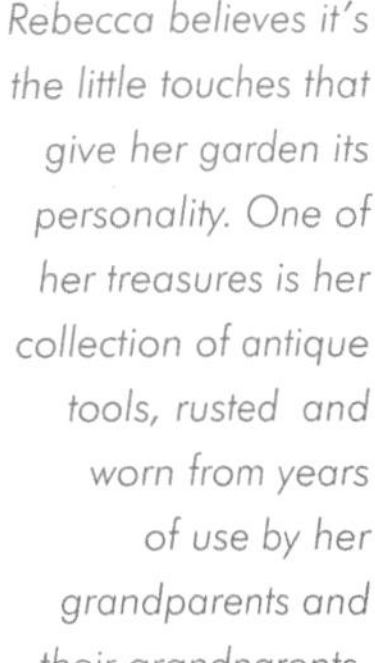

Rebecca believes it's the little touches that give her garden its personality. One of her treasures is her collection of antique tools, rusted and worn from years of use by her grandparents and their grandparents.

About the Authors

Meet Susan

Susan Morrison is a landscape designer, garden writer, and Master Gardener based in Northern California. Her design philosophy is simple: create beautiful, sustainable gardens that fit her clients' lifestyles. In addition to writing for traditional media publications such as *Fine Gardening*, Susan blogs about her life as a garden designer and shares her challenges and successes as a home gardener at "Blue Planet Garden Blog."

An early convert to the value of social media, Susan connects with gardeners from all over the world via Twitter and Facebook, and is a founding member of the Lawn Reform Coalition and the Garden Designers Roundtable. As a Master Gardener and Bay-Friendly Qualified Design Professional, Susan is active in the gardening community and speaks regularly on sustainable design principles. She is a member of the Association of Professional Landscape Designers and has served on the California Chapter Board of Directors.

Follow Susan on Twitter @susanlmorrison.
Read Susan's blog at www.blueplanetgarden.com.
View her design portfolio at www.celandscapedesign.com.

Susan's favorite part of her small suburban garden is this cozy corner. With just enough space for two lounge chairs, it's the perfect spot for relaxing and reading on warm summer evenings.